Fundamentals of
Office 365
2016 Edition

Kevin Wilson

Elluminet Press

www.elluminetpress.com

Fundamentals of Office 365: 2016 Edition

Publisher: Elluminet Press
Director: Kevin Wilson
Lead Editor: Steven Ashmore
Technical Reviewer: Mike Taylor, Robert Ashcroft
Copy Editors: Joanne Taylor, James Marsh
Proof Reader: Robert Price
Indexer: James Marsh
Cover Designer: Kevin Wilson

eBook versions and licenses are also available for most titles. Any source code or other supplementary materials referenced by the author in this text is available to readers at

www.elluminetpress.com/resources

For detailed information about how to locate your book's source code, go to

www.elluminetpress.com/resources

Table of Contents

About the Author

Kevin Wilson, a practicing computer engineer and tutor, has had a passion for gadgets, cameras, computers and technology for many years.

After graduating with masters in computer science, software engineering & multimedia systems, he has worked in the computer industry supporting and working with many different types of computer systems, worked in education running specialist lessons on film making and visual effects for young people. He has also worked as an IT Tutor, has taught in colleges in South Africa and as a tutor for adult education in England.

His books were written in the hope that it will help people to use their computer with greater understanding, productivity and efficiency. To help students and people in countries like South Africa who have never used a computer before. It is his hope that they will get the same benefits from computer technology as we do.

Acknowledgements

Thanks to all the staff at Luminescent Media & Elluminet Press for their passion, dedication and hard work in the preparation and production of this book.

To all my friends and family for their continued support and encouragement in all my writing projects.

To all my colleagues, students and testers who took the time to test procedures and offer feedback on the book

Finally thanks to you the reader for choosing this book. I hope it helps you to use your computer with greater ease.

What is Office 365

Office 365 is a subscription-based version of Microsoft Office 2016.

Unlike any of the traditional Office suites such as Office 2010, Office 365 allows you to install Office applications on up to five different computers. It includes some additional features, such as Office on Demand, 15GB - 1TB of additional online storage space through OneDrive, and the option to install Office 2016 on Mac computers.

Office 365 subscription guarantees that you'll be able to upgrade to the latest version of Office whenever it's available at no additional cost, which can save you a lot of money over time. Office 365 can be paid by either an annual or monthly subscription fee.

Office Packages

There are a number of different options and packages available depending on what your needs are.

Office 365 Home - can be installed on 5 PCs or Macs plus up to 5 mobile devices. This package is aimed at home users with more than one computer. The package includes Word, Excel, PowerPoint, Outlook, OneNote, Access and publisher. Also comes with 1TB of OneDrive space for each user.

Office 365 Personal - Has pretty much the same as Office 365 Home, except you can only install it on 1 PC or Mac and 1 Mobile device.

Office Home & Student - can be installed on one PC only and includes, Word, Excel, PowerPoint and OneNote. This is a one off payment rather than a subscription.

Office Home & Business - can be installed on one PC only and is mostly the same as Office Home & Student, except it comes with Outlook.

Office Professional - can be installed on one PC and is aimed more at business users, the package includes, Word, Excel, PowerPoint, OneNote, Outlook, publisher and Access.

Here is a comparison summary according to Microsoft's website.

	Office 365 Home	Office 365 Personal	Office Home & Student 2016	Office Home & Business 2016	Office Professional 2016
	£7.99 per month	£5.99 per month	£119.99	£229.99	£389.99
	£7.99 per month ▼	£5.99 per month ▼	Buy now	Buy now	Buy now
	Buy now	Buy now			
	Try for free	Try for free			
Purchase options	Subscription (monthly or yearly)	Subscription (monthly or yearly)	One-time purchase	One-time purchase	One-time purchase
Fully installed Office applications Word, Excel, PowerPoint, OneNote	✓ Also Outlook, Publisher, Access ⓘ	✓ Also Outlook, Publisher, Access ⓘ	✓	✓ Also Outlook	✓ Also Outlook, Publisher, Access
Installations available ⓘ	5 PCs or Macs	1 PC or Mac	1 PC	1 PC	1 PC
Tablets and phones ⓘ Get the optimized Office experience on your tablets and phones	✓ 5 tablets and 5 phones	✓ 1 tablet and 1 phone			
Offline storage Save documents to your PC or Mac	✓	✓	✓	✓	✓
OneDrive cloud storage Save documents online and access them from nearly anywhere	✓ 1 TB storage each for up to 5 users	✓ 1 TB storage for 1 user	✓ 15 GB	✓ 15 GB	✓ 15 GB

Which Package is Right for Me?

To help you decide, take some time to think about the features that are most important to you and how they fit into your budget. Below are some questions you may want to ask yourself:

- If you just need Word, Excel, and PowerPoint - the core Office applications, it may be best to buy Office Home & Student, since it's the cheapest option over the long term. This one is a one off payment, so it is unlikely you would get any of the updates in the future, but can only be installed on one machine

- If you need the more advanced applications such as Access, Publisher, Outlook Email or OneDrive storage then Office 365 Personal is a good option, but can only be installed on one machine. Also comes with 1TB of space on OneDrive.

- If you need to install Office on more than one computer. If your household has several computers, Office 365 Home subscription is a good option. You can install the Office Suite on up to 5 PCs or Macs and 5 mobile devices such as iPads, kindles, iPhones etc. Also comes with 1TB of space on OneDrive.

- Will I do a lot of editing on the go? If you use a lot of public computers at libraries or business centres, or on your iPad while travelling on the train for example, Office 365 Home may be your best option, since it includes Access to the Office Apps for mobile devices, Office on Demand and Web based versions of the Office applications.

Here is a summary from Microsoft's website

Home and Personal

5 PCs/Macs/Tablets	1 PC/Mac/Tablet	1 PC only	1 Mac only

Office 365 Home

For 5 PCs or Macs plus 5 tablets, including iPad, Android, or Windows[1]
• 1TB online storage per user for up to 5 users[3,5]
• 60 minutes of Skype calls per month[4]
• Ongoing access to updates
• Free technical support

£79.99 incl. VAT per year
£7.99 incl. VAT per month

★★★★ (78)

Suite includes[2]:

- Word
- Excel
- PowerPoint
- OneNote
- Outlook
- Publisher
- Access
- OneDrive
- Skype

Office 365 Personal

For 1 PC or Mac plus 1 tablet, including iPad, Android, or Windows[1]
• 1TB online storage for 1 user[3]
• 60 minutes monthly Skype calls for 1 user[4]
• Ongoing access to updates
• Free technical support

£59.99 incl. VAT per year
£5.99 incl. VAT per month

★★★ (23)

Suite includes[2]:

- Word
- Excel
- PowerPoint
- OneNote
- Outlook
- Publisher
- Access
- OneDrive
- Skype

Office Home and Student 2013

For 1 PC only [1]
• Store files in the cloud with OneDrive [3]
• View, share or edit your documents online
• Great new Word and Excel templates

£109.99 incl. VAT

★★★ (10)

Suite includes[2]:

- Word
- Excel
- PowerPoint
- OneNote

Office for Mac Home and Student 2011

For 1 Mac only [1]
• Store files in the cloud with OneDrive [3]
• View, share or edit your documents online
• Great new Word and Excel templates

£109.99 incl. VAT

★★★ (7)

Suite includes[2]:

- Word
- Excel
- PowerPoint

What is the Cloud?

Cloud computing is about running applications over the Internet and being able to access your files from wherever you may be; at your desk, on a train, in a coffee shop, airport and so on using a variety of different devices. These could be laptops, desktops, mobile phones or tablets.

Microsoft Office 365 is an example of a cloud service and utilises cloud computing for storage allowing you can run applications such as Word, Excel, PowerPoint, and OneNote over the internet.

Some other major examples are Google Drive and Apple iCloud.

When you run programs from the hard drive on your computer, it's called local storage. Everything is stored on your computer.

With cloud computing, you access your data and run your applications over the Internet.

These applications, services and data are stored on large server farms and are managed by the cloud service.

Your OneDrive files are stored on a server in this server farm rather than locally on your computer.

In the photograph above, there can be about 30 or more servers stacked up in each cabinet and hundreds of cabinets filling entire rooms serving millions of people who subscribe to the service.

The advantage is, you can log in and access your files anywhere on the internet and your files are backed up by the cloud service, so should your computer fail, your files will still be on your OneDrive.

Setting up Office 365

To begin setting up Office 365, you need to log onto Microsoft's website, purchase a subscription to Office, then download and install the software on your computer.

In this chapter we will take a look at how to get up and running quickly.

We will also take a look at creating a Microsoft Account so you can use Microsoft's online services such as OneDrive and email.

As well as access the apps on your phone, iPad or tablet computer.

So lets begin by navigating over to the Microsoft Store.

Purchasing Office Online

First open your web browser and go to Microsoft office website

http://products.office.com

In this example we are purchasing the home premium version. If you want to download a different version change it by clicking 'office products' and selecting the version from the drop down box. The procedure is the same.

From the home page select 'For Home'

Click buy now in the Office 365 Home column.

You can either pay a monthly subscription or pay an annual cost. Choose depending on your budget.

Paying monthly will spread the cost over the year rather than paying one lump sum.

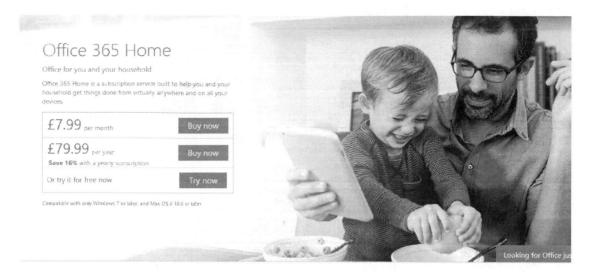

Select 'buy now'. In this example I am going to pay monthly. Click 'review and checkout'

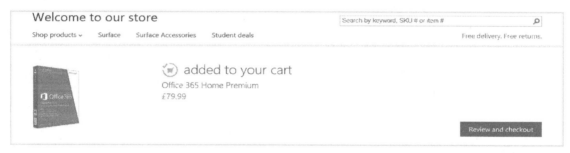

Click 'next'. Sometimes depending on your country you might also see 'checkout'. Click to confirm your order.

Once you have done that you will be prompted to sign in with your Microsoft account.

If you are using Windows 8 or 10 you will probably already have a Microsoft account that you created when you set up your machine.

This is usually the username/email and password you used to sign into Windows.

If so enter these details into the screen below.

If this is not the case then you can quickly create one.

Create a Microsoft Account

To set up a Microsoft Account you need to open a new web browser. To do this, hold down the Control (ctrl) key on your keyboard and tap N (don't hold the 'N' key down). Or click your web browser icon.

Go to the following website

`http://signup.live.com`

You will see a form asking for your details.

Create an account

You can use any email address as the username for your new Microsoft account, including addresses from Outlook.com, Yahoo! or Gmail. If you already sign in to a Windows PC, tablet or phone, Xbox Live, Outlook.com or SkyDrive, use that account to sign in.

Name

| First name | Surname |

Username

| someone@example.com |

Or get a new email address

Create password

| |

8-character minimum; case-sensitive

Re-enter password

| |

Country/region

| United Kingdom ⌄ |

Postal Code

| |

Date of birth

| Day ⌄ | Month ⌄ | Year ⌄ |

Gender

| Select one ⌄ |

Enter all the required details in the fields then scroll down the form.

Once you have filled in all the details click 'create account' at the bottom

Setup your Payment Method

Go back to your browser with your office store. To do this, hold down Alt and tap Tab (don't hold Tab key down).

Sign in with the account you just created

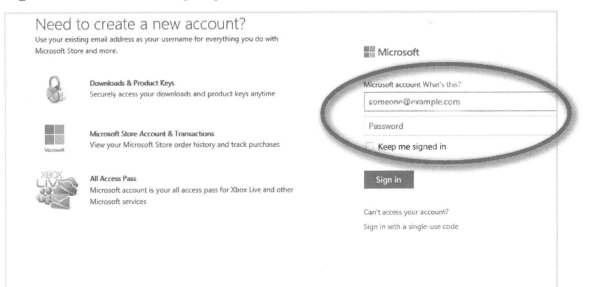

You will be prompted to enter your payment details. If you have purchased from the Microsoft store before then you can choose to pay with an existing card or you can add a different card number.

Enter your information in all the fields then click next at the bottom of the screen then review and confirm your order.

Downloading Office 2016 Suite

If Office doesn't update itself automatically, you can update your Office installation on your computer by navigating to the following website and loggin into your Office 365 account.

office.com

Sign in with your Microsoft Account details

Scroll down to the bottom of the page and click on 'My Account'

From 'My Office Account' page click 'install'

Click 'run' when prompted by your web browser

The Office installer will run and begin downloading the necessary files to install Office 2016 on your computer.

This can take a while to complete depending on the speed of your computer and your internet connection.

The Installer will run once it has finished downloading. You may need to enter your computer's password you used to log into Windows.

Once Office is installed, click 'close'

You will be able to find your Office 2016 Apps installed on your start menu. You may have to go to 'app apps' if you don't see any tiles or shortcuts on your start menu.

If this is not your computer and belongs to someone else in the family, open up an office application such as Microsoft word and select a blank document.

If this is your own computer then you can skip this step.

Click file from the top left hand side and from the screen that appears, shown below, select 'account'.

In the main window, Click on 'sign out'

This will allow that person to sign in using their own Microsoft account, rather than using yours.

Exchange Email on your iPhone

Tap Settings > Mail, Contacts, Calendars > Add Account.

Tap Microsoft Exchange.

Domain box can be left blank.

Enter your Microsoft account email and password

Tap Next on the upper-right corner of the screen.

The mail app will automatically detect settings for server names etc.

If your iPhone doesn't automatically detect the settings you can enter them manually

> Server name for IMAP and POP is **outlook.office365.com**
>
> Server name for SMTP is **smtp.office365.com**.
>
> Exchange ActiveSync server name is **outlook.office365.com**

These settings can be used if you are using the latest version of Office 365.

Select what information you want to synchronize or copy between your phone and Office 356. Eg, Mail, Contacts, and Calendar information.

If you're prompted to create a passcode, tap Continue and type in a numeric passcode.

If you don't set up a passcode, you can't view your email account on your iPhone.

Set up Email on Windows Phone

On Start, swipe left to the App list, select Settings, and then select email accounts.

Select add an account

Select Outlook.

Enter your email address and password, then select Sign in. Windows Phone will set up your email account automatically.

If your phone doesn't automatically detect the settings you can enter them manually

> Exchange ActiveSync server name is **outlook.office365.com**

These settings can be used if you are using the latest version of Office 365.

Select what information you want to synchronize or copy between your phone and Office 356. Eg by default, Mail, Contacts, and Calendar information are synchronized.

Setting up Outlook Desktop App

When you first start the Outlook application you will be asked to enter your email address, password and sometimes your mail settings.

Click Next, then click Yes to the question "Do you want to set up Outlook to connect to an email account?"

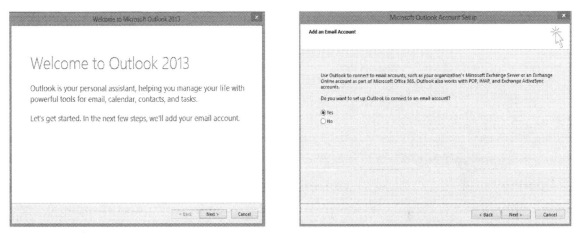

Then click Next to get to the following screen (Add Account). In "Auto Account Setup" enter your name, email address and Password for your Office 365 account.

Click Next. Microsoft Outlook will scan the email address you have entered and enter all the server and mail settings for you.

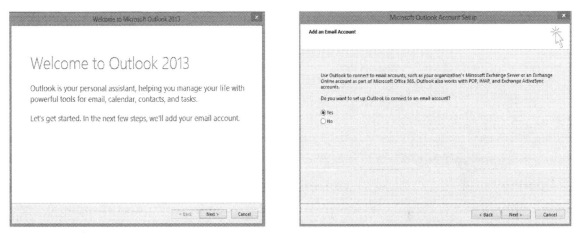

Office Apps for iOS

Microsoft has released its office apps for the iPad & iPhone. You can find the apps on Microsoft's web site using the following link

http://products.office.com/mobile

Or search on the App Store on your iPad

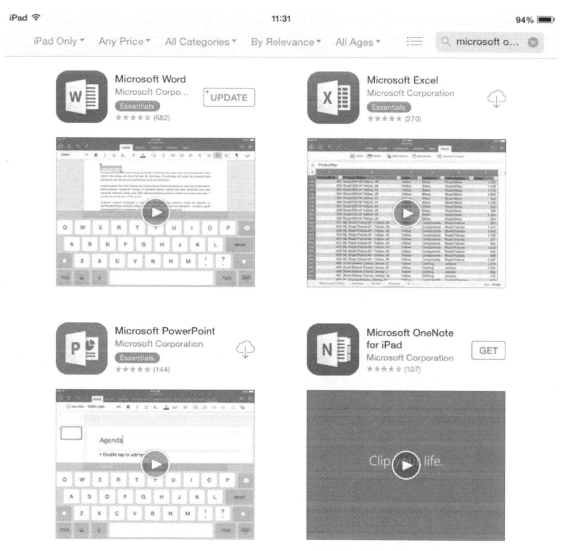

Tap 'Get' (or the cloud icon) to download the app.

Setting up OneDrive on iOS

You can access your files on OneDrive by downloading the app from the app store on your iPad

Type OneDrive into the search field on the top right of the app store.

You will need an apple store account to download the apps.

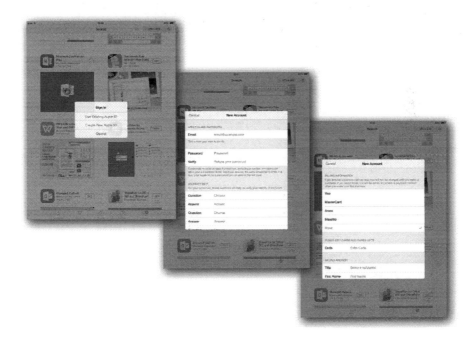

When you tap on an app to download it the Apple App Store will ask you for your Apple ID, enter these details if you have them.

If you don't have an Apple ID then tap 'Create New Apple ID' from the sign in options. Then enter your details as shown above.

Setting up OneDrive on PC

You can set up OneDrive by installing the app on your iPad or Android device and by downloading the app on your PC, Mac or Laptop.

If you have Windows 8 or 10 then OneDrive will already be installed.

If you have Windows 7 or a Mac On your PC/Laptop/Mac, open your web browser and go to

```
http://onedrive.live.com
```

If you have already created a Microsoft Account, click download in the top of the screen

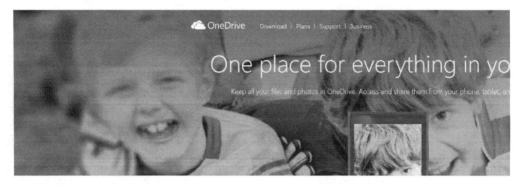

Select your operating system (eg Mac or Windows) from the choices listed along the top

On the left hand side under 'OneDrive', click 'Download Now'

If your company or school/college gave you an account, select 'OneDrive for business' instead.

When prompted click 'Run'

Enter your Microsoft Account details when prompted.

You will be able to access your files in file explorer by going to the OneDrive folder.

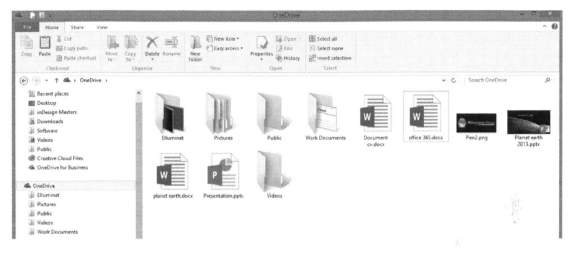

Chapter 3

Office 365 Online

Office 365 has a wealth of online applications. You can use office through your web browser using web apps, or you can stream live versions of office applications using office on demand.

You can synchronise all your files and keep them in the cloud using OneDrive so you can access your files wherever you go.

This is a useful feature, for example, if you have Office installed on your machine at work/college you can synchronise all your files with your computer at home.

You can also get your files on your iPad, iPhone, or Android tablet. Access them on any PC, laptop or net-book computer.

You can also run your favourite Office apps over the internet using a web browser.

Lets begin by taking a look at Microsoft Office web apps.

Web Apps

With your office 365 subscription you can access your favourite office applications such as Word, Excel, Outlook through your web browser.

This can be useful if you need to edit a document or perhaps give a PowerPoint presentation on a computer that doesn't have office installed or the same version of office.

Open your web browser and navigate to

office.com

Click Sign in on the top right corner and enter your Microsoft account details

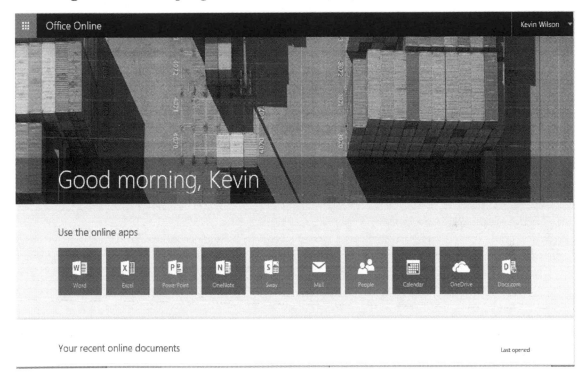

From here you can open Word, Outlook email, OneNote, PowerPoint, see your Outlook calendar, open Excel or your OneDrive.

You can use these applications in the same way you would your ordinary office applications.

Your recently opened documents are listed down the left hand side. If the file is not there click 'Open from OneDrive' on the bottom left.

To start a new document, click either a blank document or one of the many pre designed templates.

The web apps are integrated into OneDrive and open automatically when you select documents, Excel spreadsheets or PowerPoint presentations.

Microsoft Sway

Sway is a presentation tool that allows you to drag and drop files such as images or online videos from social media into presentations, reports, newsletters and personal stories.

You can either use the app on your phone/tablet or using a web browser by navigating to the following website.

`sway.com`

You can download the App from the App Store

You can begin creating Sways by typing in a Title where it says 'Title you Sway'.

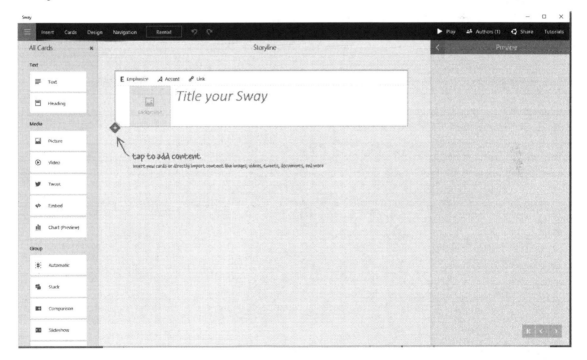

In this example, I'm going to type in the title: "Planet Earth". Sway will begin searching for information on the web about planet earth. If you click 'Insert' on the top menu, you can insert all different types of media.

In this case Sway has searched the web for images and information on the title I entered earlier, "Planet Earth".

If I click where it says 'suggested', I can select the sources of information. This can be from youtube, 'my albums' on facebook, a bing/google image search, from my own camera or upload from my computer.

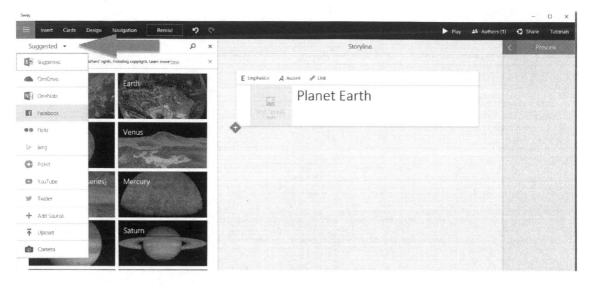

I can now start to drag the images and information I want into the time-line on the right hand side. I can also type in text, insert videos.

Mail

You can access your mail through a web browser. If you are already signed into your account click on the icon for mail

OR

If not open your web browser and navigate to

`outlook.com`

Sign in with your Microsoft Account details.

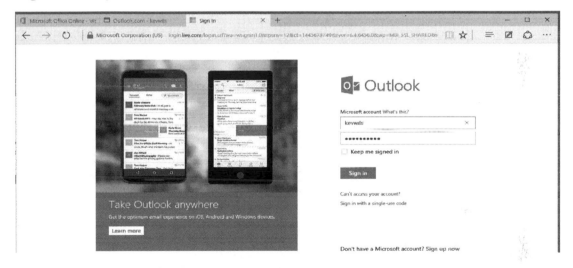

Once signed in you'll see your main screen.

Calendar

You can access your calendar through a web browser. If you are already signed into your account click on the icon for mail

Or open your web browser and navigate to

`calendar.live.com`

Add events either by double clicking on the date in the calendar or by clicking 'new' and selecting 'event'

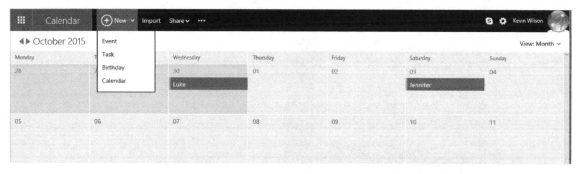

In the page that appears, enter dates and times, name of appointment, eg: 'coffee with kate'. Add a location or address. Set a reminder, 15 mins before appointment, a day before, etc. Once you are done click 'save'

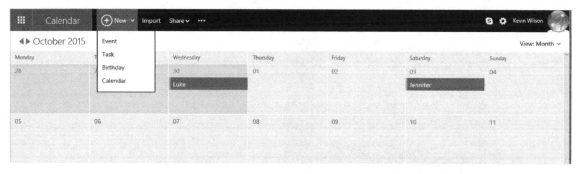

People

Click the people icon on your homepage or navigate to

```
people.live.com
```

The people app is equivalent to your contacts list or address book. Click on a name in your contact list down the left hand side of the screen. That person's details will appear in the pane on the right.

Click/tap on the email address to send a new message, or click/tap the phone to call the person.

You can add a new contact by clicking/tapping on 'New'

Fill in the person's details.

You can also import contacts from your social media and other email accounts. Do this by clicking 'manage', then 'Add people'

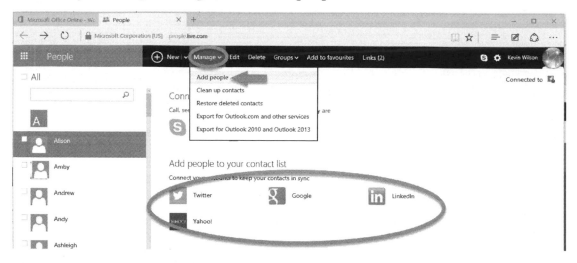

Click on the icons circled above to import contacts from those accounts. You will need your account details for this.

Docs

Docs is an online tool that allows you to publish and share PowerPoint, Word, Excel, PDF documents and Sways.

Click on the docs icon

or open your web browser and navigate to

docs.com

From here click 'sign in' on the top right of the screen. Enter your Microsoft Account email and password.

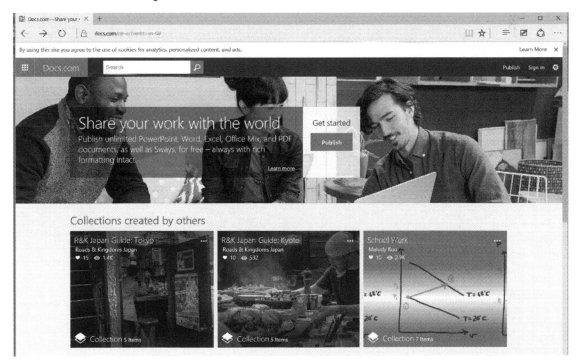

Once you are signed in, click the 'publish' button.

From here you can upload a PowerPoint presentation, PDF, Excel sheet or a Word document.

You can upload them from your local computer or device or import them from OneDrive. I store all my files on OneDrive, so in this example I'm going to select OneDrive as shown below.

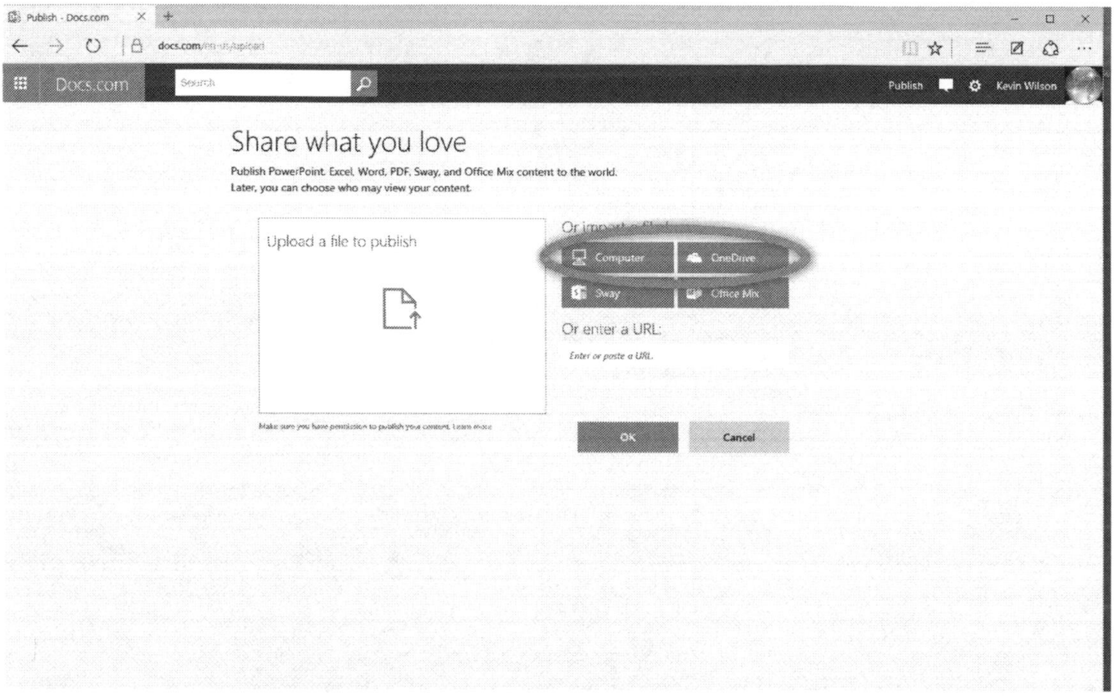

From here, select the file you want to publish.

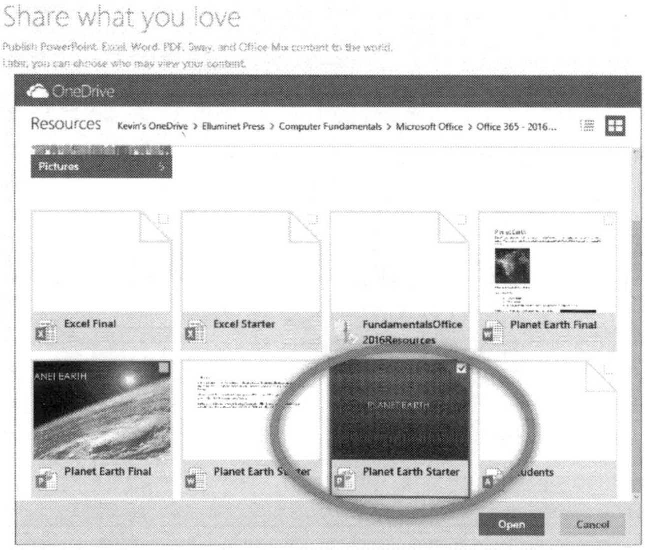

Add a title, author and a brief description

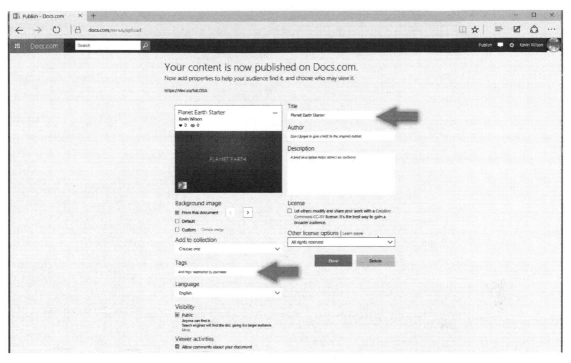

Once you have filled in all the details, click 'done'.

You can now share the link to your publication with friends and colleagues on social media and email.

When a friend or colleague follows the link, they will be able to view the document.

Office Mix

Microsoft Office Mix is an add-on for Powerpoint that allows teachers and students to create interactive multimedia presentations featuring audio, video, slides, inking on slides, interactive activities, and interactive assessments.

To download it, open your web browser and navigate to

`mix.office.com`

From here click 'get office mix' on the top right of the screen.

Click 'sign in with a Microsoft Account'

Click on 'run' when prompted. If you don't get the prompt click where it says 'click here' on the web page.

Once the installer has finished, you will see a new ribbon menu in PowerPoint.

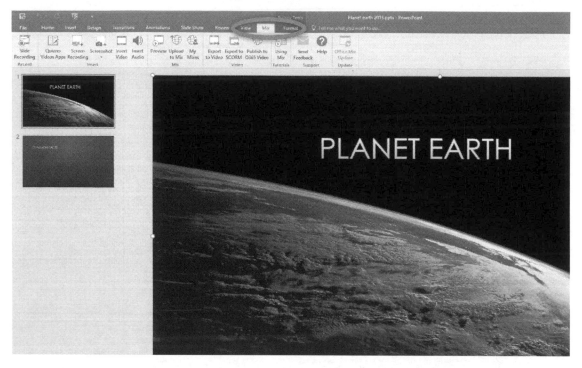

Using OneDrive on the Web

OneDrive is online storage you can use as your own personal online hard drive dubbed cloud storage and is part of Office 365 and Microsoft Accounts.

OneDrive is integrated into Windows 8.1 and 10 to allow users to save files to the cloud with just a few taps or clicks.

When you create a document with one of the Web Apps, it is saved to your OneDrive. You can store other files there, too such as photos.

Since Web Apps and OneDrive are based in the cloud, you can access them from any device with an internet connection, at any time.

To access your OneDrive from any computer, open your web browser and go to

```
http://onedrive.live.com
```

From here you can see all your files you have saved to your OneDrive

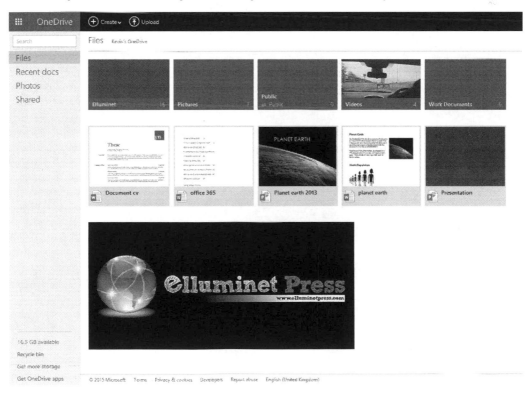

Editing Files

Click on any document to open it in the appropriate office application.

If you need to edit the document, click on 'edit document' on the top left of the screen. This will give you a choice to open the document in the application installed on your computer or edit it in the web based application.

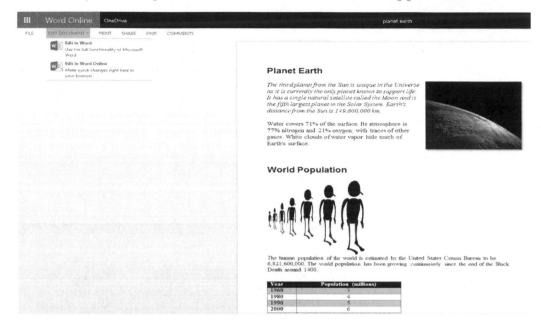

In this example, I am opening up a Word document. If Word is not installed on my local computer then I'd click 'Edit in Word Online'

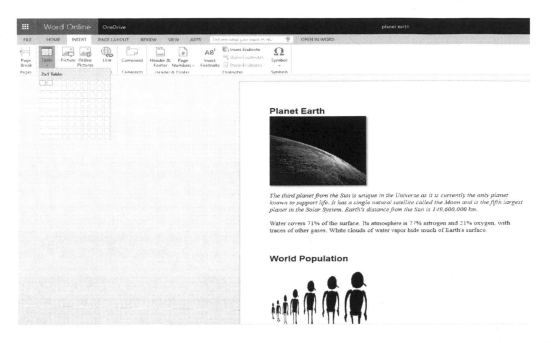

This will allow you to edit the document. Any changes you make are saved back to your OneDrive.

Uploading Files

You can upload files from the computer you are using at anytime using OneDrive in your web browser.

To do this click 'Upload'

In the dialog box that appears, select the file you want to upload. Then click 'Open'

Organising Files

You can organise your files into directories using OneDrive. This helps to keep files together.

If you move your mouse over a thumbnail of the file you want, a small check box will appear in the top right, click this box to select the file.

You will also notice, along the top new menu items will appear. These options allow you to open the file, download a copy, share with friends or facebook, manage your file (rename, move to another folder).

To create a new folder, right click on some empty space and from the pop up menu that appears select 'Create', then click 'Folder'

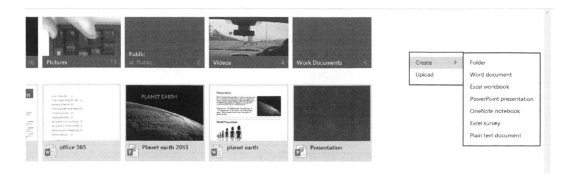

To move files, you can click and drag them into the appropriate folders.

OneDrive on your Desktop

You can edit your documents, or create new documents and save them to your OneDrive where you will be able to access them from your PC by going to your OneDrive folder in file explorer.

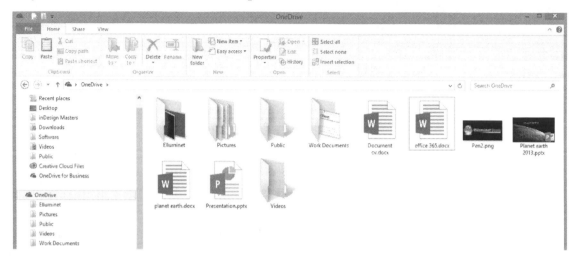

Double clicking on any of the documents will open them using the Office applications installed on your PC. You can edit them in the usual way.

Uploading Files

You can upload files from your PC using the windows file explorer

Locate the file on your computer that you wish to upload to your OneDrive using Windows File Explorer, in this case the file I want is located in the Documents library.

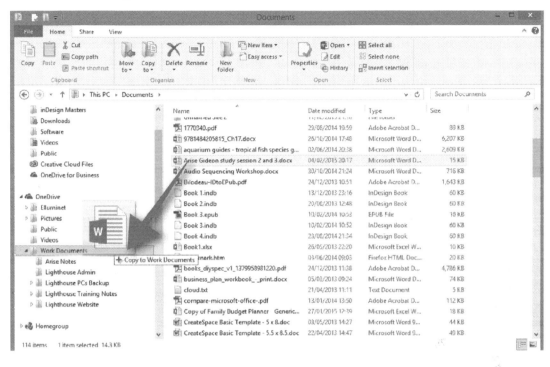

Click and drag the file to the OneDrive folder as shown in the image above.

Searching for Files

If you know the names of the documents you can use the search feature to locate them quickly.

Select the location to search in. In this example I want to search for my 'Gideon' files in the documents library.

So select documents under the 'libraries' section in the left hand pane as shown below.

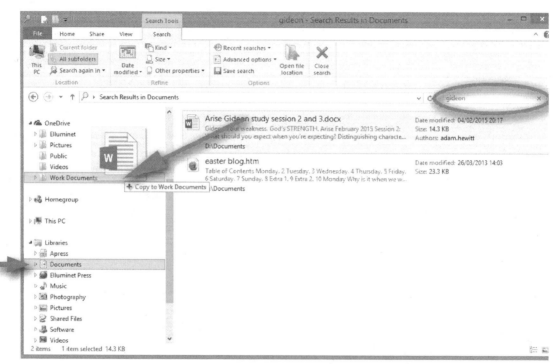

Then type the name of the document in the 'search documents' field, circled above. This will bring up a list of all documents containing the word you typed.

To add them to your OneDrive just drag and drop the file as show above.

Using your iPad

Once you have set up your iPad as in previous chapter, the Apps will be available on your home screen

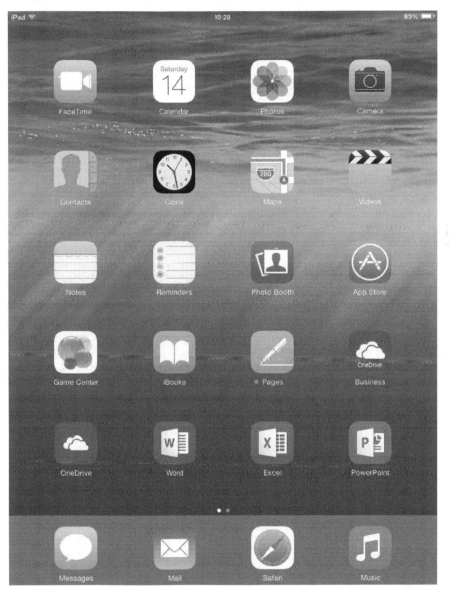

Accessing your Files

To access your files you can find them using the OneDrive App. This allows you to see all your files and documents you have saved to your OneDrive.

Tap the OneDrive icon on your home screen. If it's the first time you have used OneDrive, enter your Microsoft account email address and password when prompted.

Once logged in, you will see a screen similar to the following

You can open any of your files by tapping on their icons.

Upload Files to OneDrive

You can upload files from your iPad to OneDrive. These are usually photos you have taken with the built in camera. Any documents you create with the office apps on your iPad are automatically saved to your OneDrive.

To upload an image tap the ooo icon on the top right of the screen then follow the sequence below

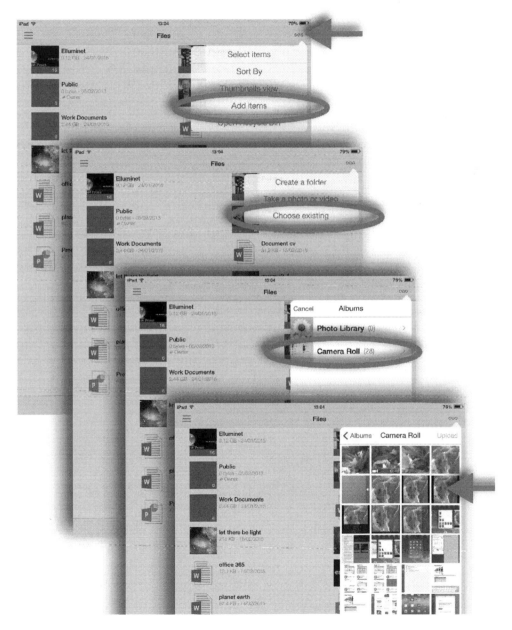

You can select multiple photos by tapping on the ones you want to upload.

Editing Files on iPad

If this is the first time using the app, you will need to sign in using your Microsoft Account details. If the sign in box doesn't appear, tap 'sign in' on the top left.

Once you have logged into your account, you will see something similar to the following.

From here you can create new documents or open documents saved on your OneDrive.

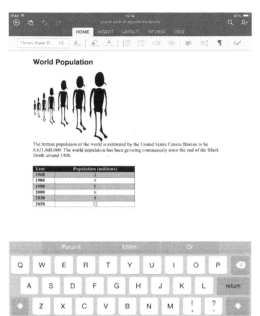

Microsoft Word 2016

Microsoft Word is a word processing application that allows you to create many different types of document, from letters, Resumes/CVs to greetings cards, posters and flyers all from a library of customisable templates or from scratch.

Word 2016 gives you the ability to do more with your word processing projects, with the introduction of several enhanced features, such as the ability to create and collaborate on documents online using OneDrive.

Your first step in creating a document in Word 2016 is to choose whether to start from a blank document or to let a template do much of the work for you.

From then on, the basic steps in creating and sharing documents are the same.

Powerful editing and reviewing tools help you work with others to make your document perfect

Lets begin by launching Word 2016

Starting Word

The quickest way to start Microsoft Word is to search for it using the Cortana search field on the bottom left of your task bar. Type "Word 2016".

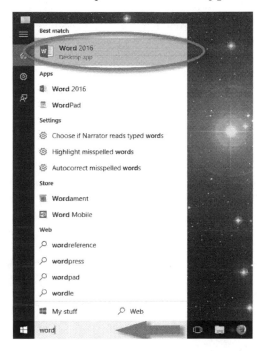

Once Word has loaded, you can select a document from a wide variety of templates, eg brochures, CVs, letters, flyers, etc. If you want to create your own just select blank. Your recently saved documents are shown on the blue pane on the left hand side.

You can also search for a particular template using the search field.

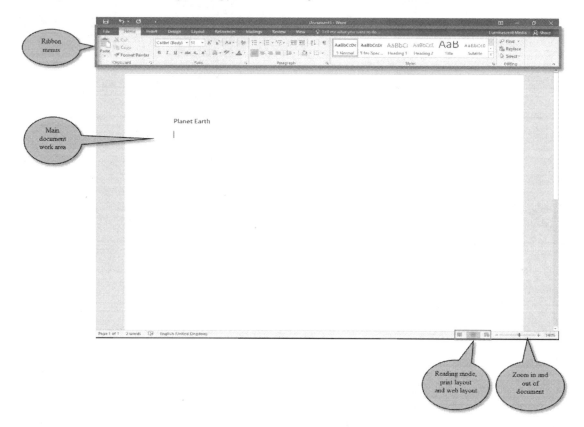

Getting Around Word

Once you select a template, you will see your main work screen.

All the tools used in Microsoft word are organised into ribbons loosely based on their function, circled above.

Lets take a closer look.

The Home Ribbon

You will find your text formatting tools here for making text bold, changing style, font, paragraph alignment etc.

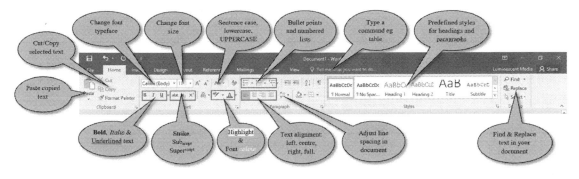

The Insert Ribbon

This is where you will find your clip-art, tables, pictures, page breaks, and pretty much anything you would want to insert into a document.

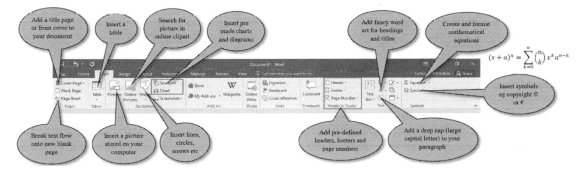

The Design Ribbon

Anything to do with pre-set themes and formatting such as headings, colours and fonts that you can apply to your document and word will automatically format your document according to the themes.

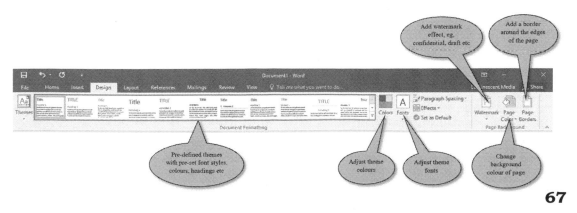

The Page Layout Ribbon

This ribbon you will find your page sizes, margins, page orientation (landscape or portrait) and anything to do with how your page is laid out.

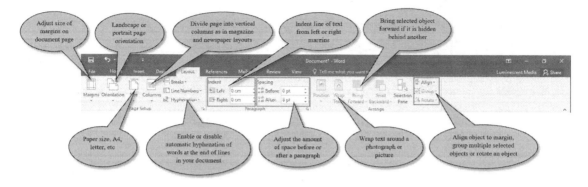

The References Ribbon

This is where you can add automatically generated tables of contents, indexes, footnotes to your documents

The Mailings Ribbon

From the mailings ribbon you can print mailing labels, print on envelopes and create mail-merge documents from a list of names & addresses.

Text Formatting

To format the document we are going to use the formatting tools. These are on the home ribbon shown below.

Using Paragraph Styles

Word has a number of paragraph styles that are useful for keeping your formatting consistent.

For example you can set a font style, size and colour for a heading or title style...

...and a different style for your text.

This makes it easier to format your document so you don't have to apply the same font style, size and colour manually every time you want to a heading.

All the styles are pre-set

To set the styles for a heading or paragraph, just highlight it with your mouse as shown below.

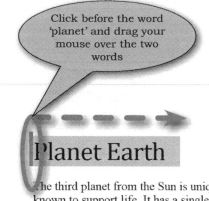

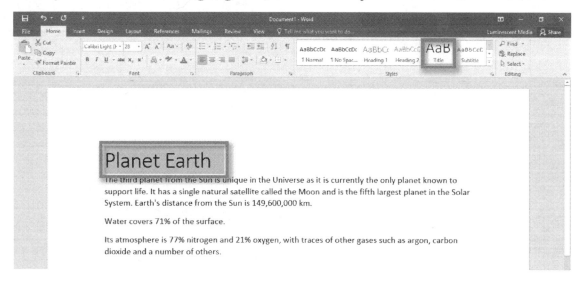

Once you have the text highlighted, click on a style from the home ribbon.

In this example I will use the title style for the heading of my document.

Bold, Italic, Underlined

You can use **bold**, *italic* or <u>underlined</u> text to emphasise certain words or paragraphs. Select the text you want to apply formatting to.

For example, I want to make the text "water", "nitrogen" and "oxygen" bold, select them with the mouse and click the bold icon on your home ribbon.

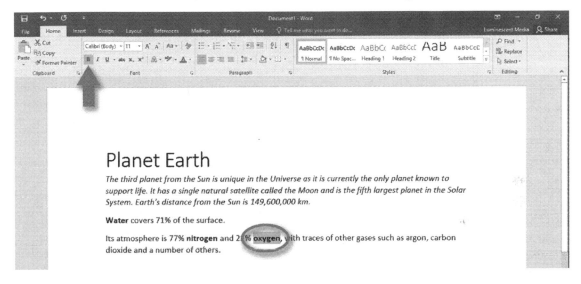

Justify Text: Left, Centred, Right, Full

You can align text to different margins.

Most text will be **left aligned** as demonstrated in this paragraph. Only the left margin is aligned, the right margin is not.

Text can also be **right aligned**
this is good for addresses on the top of letters

Text can also be **fully justified**. This means that the left and right margins are both aligned. This helps when creating documents with images as the text will line up neatly around the image.

Select the text you want to apply formatting to.

In this example, I want to make the paragraphs fully justified. This means the text is aligned both the left and right margins.

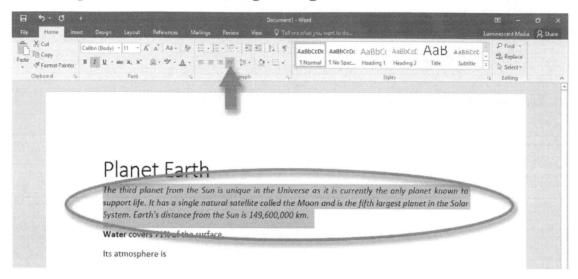

Select the text and in the home ribbon select the fully justify icon.

Bullets and Numbered Lists

Edit the document and change the sentence explaining atmospheric composition to a bullet point list. Select the text using your mouse as shown below.

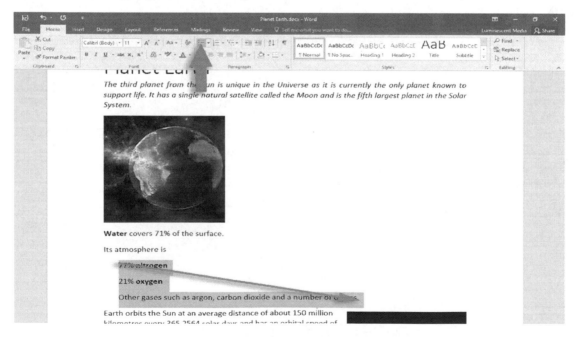

Then from your home ribbon, click the bullet points icon.

Cut, Copy & Paste

To ease editing documents, you can use copy, cut and paste to move paragraphs or pictures around in different parts of your document.

First select the paragraph below with your mouse by clicking before the word 'Earth' and dragging your mouse across the line towards the end as shown below.

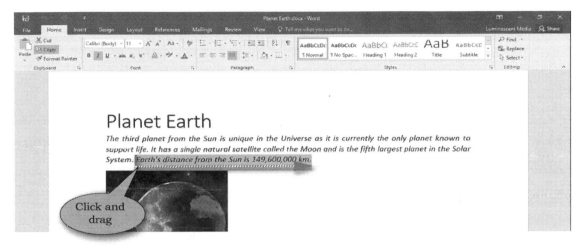

Once you have done that, click 'cut' from the left hand side of your home ribbon. This will 'cut out' the paragraph.

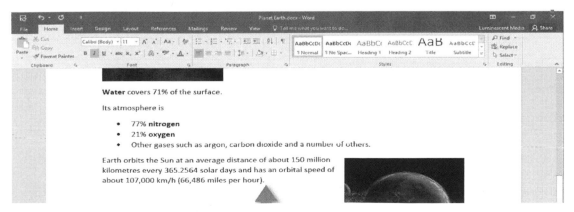

Now click on the position you want the paragraph you just cut out to be inserted.

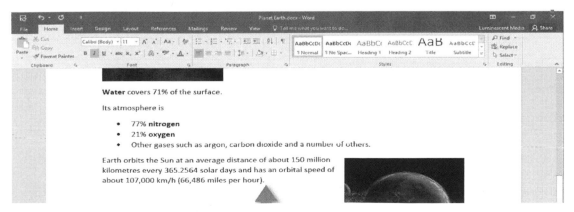

Once you have done that click 'paste' from the home ribbon. If you wanted to copy something ie make a duplicate of the text, then use the same procedure except click 'copy' instead of 'cut'.

Adding Images

Adding images to your document is easy.

There are two ways.

- Your own photos and pictures stored on your computer or OneDrive.

- Clipart. This is a large library of images that can be used in your documents.

Click on the position in your document where you want your photograph or image to appear.

Go to your insert ribbon and click on 'Pictures'

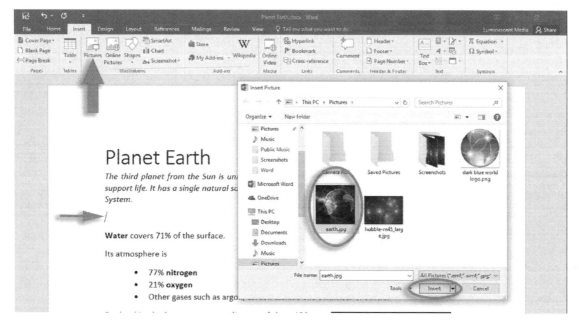

Choose the picture or photo you want from the dialog box that appears.

Click insert.

This will insert your photo into your document.

You can move the photo by clicking and dragging it to the position you want it.

You can also search for images on Google. When you download an image, make sure you save them into your pictures folder.

Follow the diagram below starting at the top left.

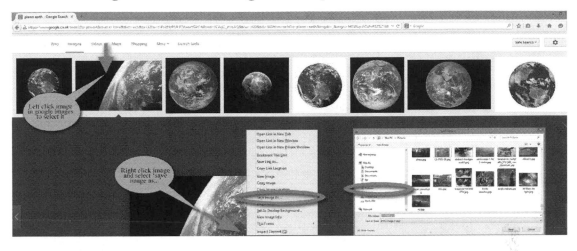

Once your image is saved into your pictures folder, you can import them into your word document using the procedure on the previous page.

Once imported into Word, you may need to resize the image, as sometimes they can come in a bit big.

To do this click on the image, you'll see small handles appear on each corner of the image.

These are called resize handles and you can use them by clicking and dragging a corner toward the centre of the image to make it smaller as shown below.

Adding Clipart

Carrying on with our document, I want to add a new section called "World Population" and I want some clipart to illustrate this. Office.com clipart library is no longer supported and has been replaced with Bing images.

First click the position in your document where you want the clipart to appear.

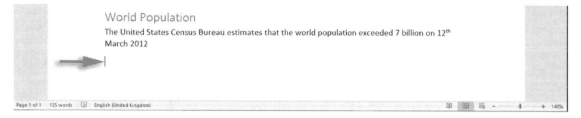

Go to your insert ribbon and click 'online pictures'.

Then in the dialog box type in what you are looking for, as shown below. In this case enter the search term 'population'.

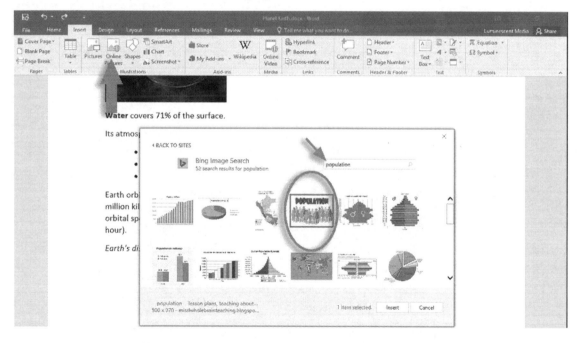

In the search results, click the image you want then click insert

World Population

The United States Census Bureau estimates that the world population exceeded 7 billion on 12th March 2012

Formatting Images

When you click on your image another ribbon appears called Format. This allows you to add effects and layout your pictures on your page.

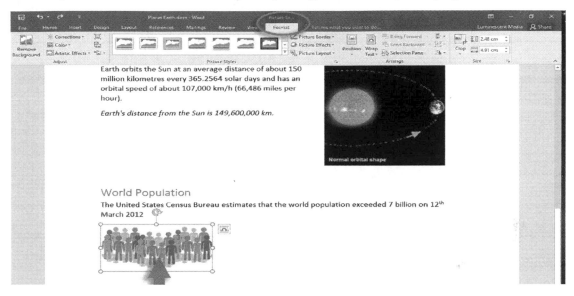

The first thing we want to do is change the text wrapping. Text wrapping enables you to surround a picture or diagram with text.

To do this, click on your image and click the format ribbon.

Click Wrap Text. Then select square. This wraps the text squarely around the image.

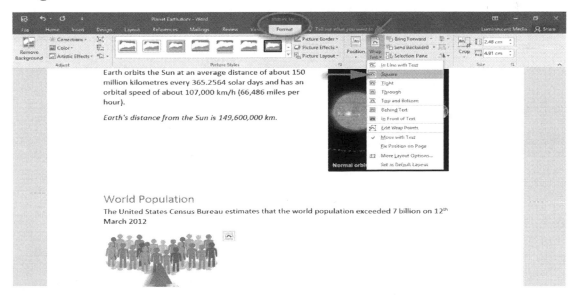

You can now move the image into the correct position, when you do this you will find the text will wrap itself around the image.

Adding Effects to Images

To add effects to your images, such as shadows and borders, click on your image then select the Format ribbon.

In this example, click on the population image.

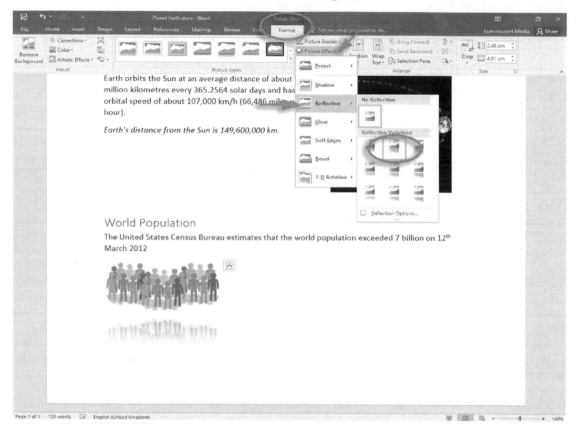

I want to create a nice reflection style to the image. To do this click 'picture effects', then 'reflection' then select a variation as shown above.

Try different effects, such as 'shadow', 'bevel' or 'glow'.

See what affect they have...

Cropping Images

If you insert an image into your document and it has unwanted parts or you want to concentrate on one particular piece of the picture you can crop your image

First insert an image from your pictures library into your document .

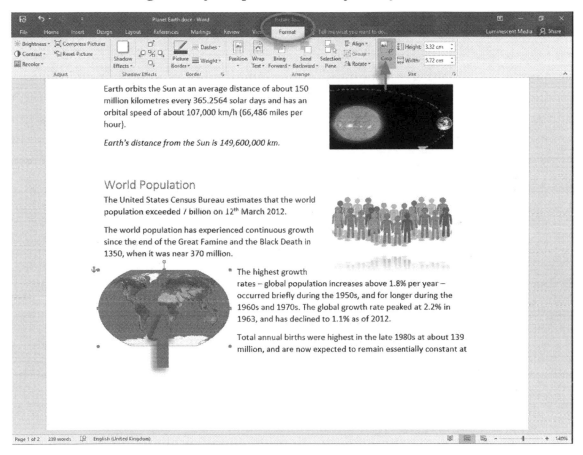

To crop, click on the image then click the format ribbon.

From the format ribbon click the crop icon.

If you look closely at your image you will see crop handles around the edges, circled below.

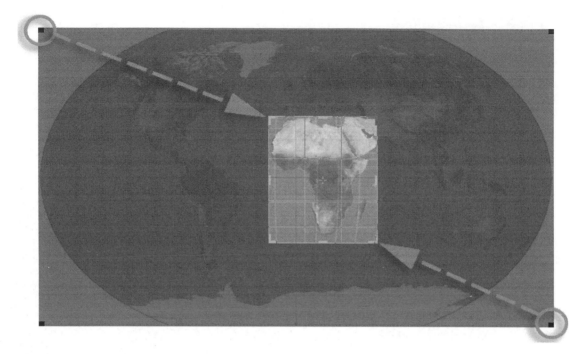

Click and drag these around the part of the image you want. Eg, I just want to show Africa in the image.

The dark grey bits will be removed to leave the bit of the image inside the crop square

Adding Tables

We have added some more text about world population to our document. Now we want to add a table to illustrate our text.

To insert a table click on your document where you want the table to appear. In this example I want it to appear just below world population paragraph.

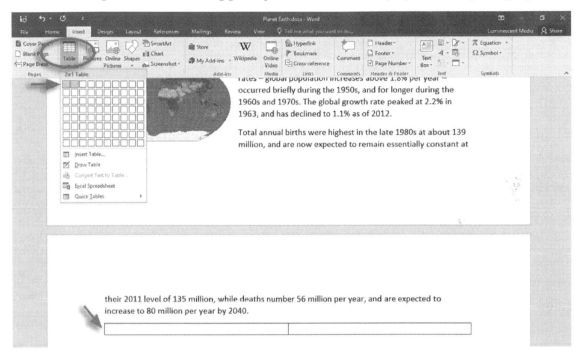

Go to your insert ribbon and select table.

In the grid that appears highlight the number of rows and columns you want. For this table, 1 row and 2 columns.

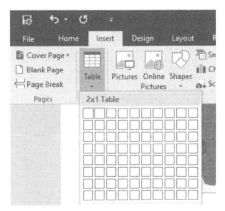

This will add a table with 1 rows & columns to your document.

Now just fill in the table. To move between cells on the table press the tab key.

When you get to the end of the row, pressing tab will insert a new row.

Country	Population
China	1,372,000,000
India	1,276,900,000
USA	321,793,000
Indonesia	252,164,800
Brazil	204,878,000

When working with tables, two new ribbons appear, design and layout.

The design tab allows you to select pre-set designs for your table such as column and row shading, borders etc.

For this table I am going to choose one with blue headings and shaded rows.

Click any cell in the table and click the design ribbon. From the designs select one you like.

Inserting Rows & Columns

To add a row, right click on the row where you want to insert. For example, I want to add a row between USA and Indonesia. So right click on Indonesia

From the drop down menu that appears, click insert.

Click 'insert above'. This will insert a row above the one you right clicked on.

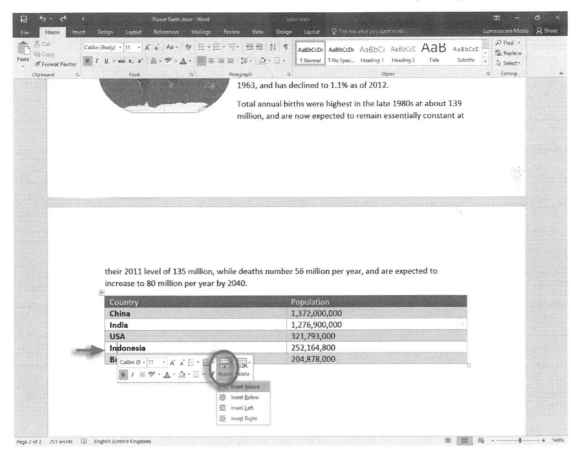

Templates

Microsoft Word has a wealth of pre-designed templates for you to use. You can find templates and layouts for letters, CV/Resumes, leaflets, flyers, reports and pretty much any kind of document you can think of.

When you start Word, you will see a screen containing thumbnails of different templates that are available.

The best way to find templates is to search for them.

In the search results, double click on the template you want to use.

In the document that opens up, notice there are a number of fields. When you click on these fields they will be highlighted in grey. These are just place-holders where you can enter your information

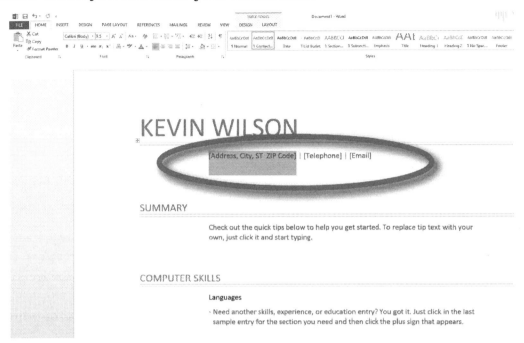

Click on these and type in your information. You will also be able to fully edit the document as normal.

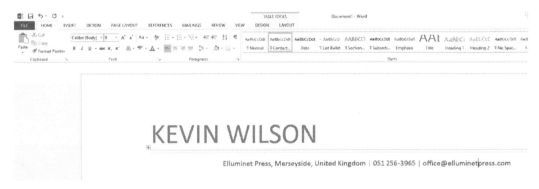

Real Time Co-Authoring

A new feature that allows authors or users to work on a document at the same time

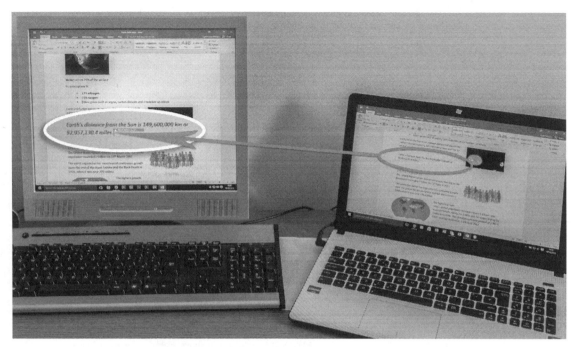

In the top right of Word there is a share button. You can share any document you are working on with friends and colleagues.

If you want to share the document you are working on, click on the share button and enter their email address.

Set 'Automatically share changes' to 'always' so your colleagues can see your changes then click 'share'.

When the other person checks their email, they will receive a message inviting them to open the document you just shared.

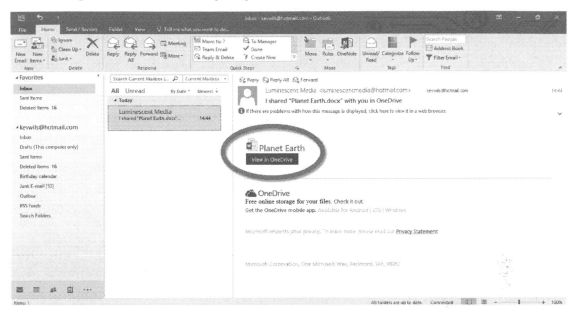

Click 'view in OneDrive'. The document will open in a web browser. Make sure you click sign in on the top right of the screen and enter your Microsoft Account details.

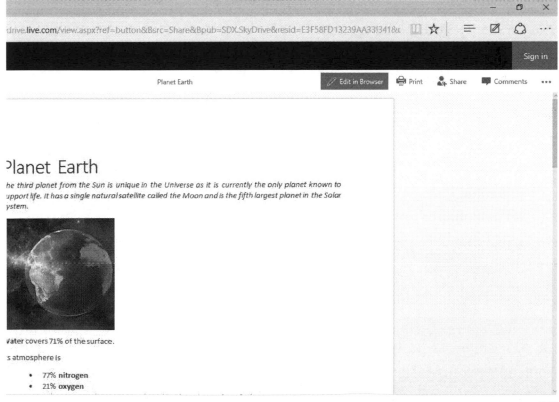

Once you have signed in, click 'edit document', then click 'edit in word'

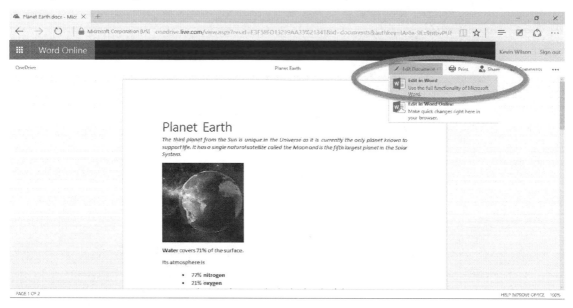

This will download the document and open it up in Word 2016 installed on your computer.

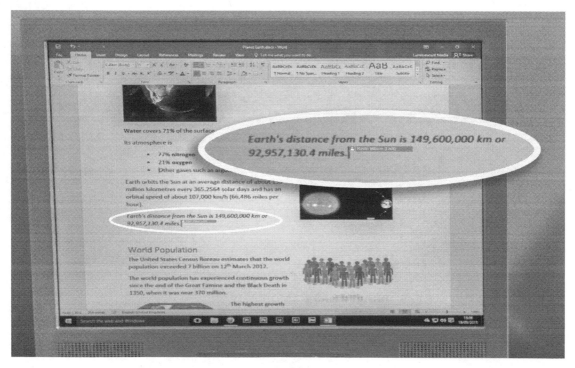

Once the document has loaded, you'll be able to see the other user editing your document. Any editing they do will be labelled with their username above the cursor as they make changes.

Insights

With insights, you can bring information in from online sources right into Word. Word can gather information from online encyclopedias, web searches and other online sources.

You can find insights by navigating over to your review ribbon. To look something up, click on a particular key word, or highlight a name or heading and click 'smart lookup'.

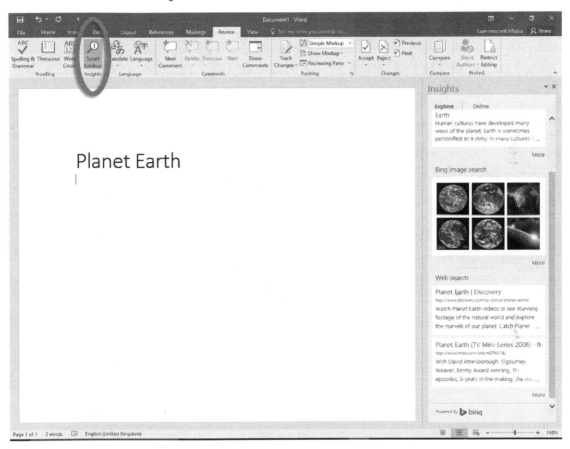

The insights bar will open on the right hand side of your screen. Here you can find images and information about your search.

Click and drag the images to your document if you choose to use them. You can also click on the links in the web searches to view more information.

Saving Documents

To save your work, click the small disk icon in the top left hand corner of the screen

In the save as screen, you need to tell word where you want to save the document.

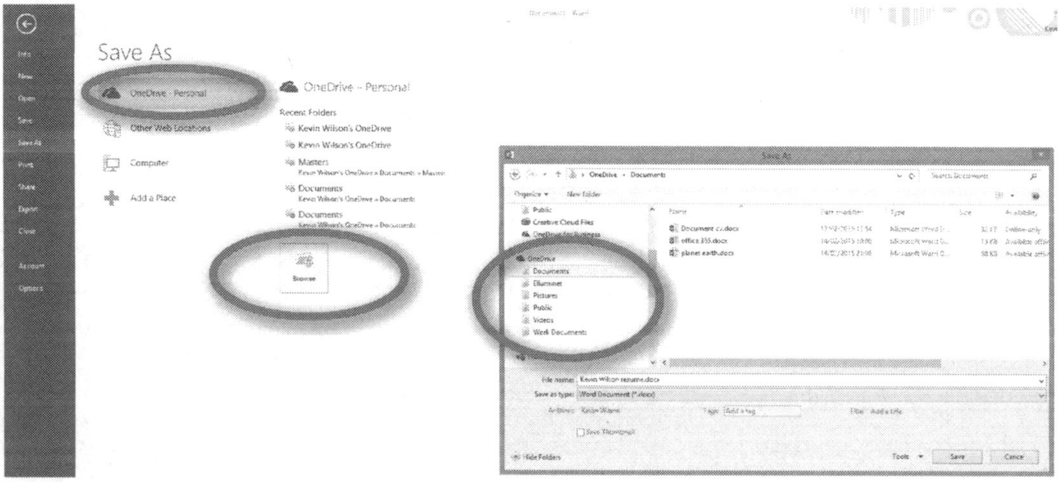

Save it onto "OneDrive Personal" and in "Documents" folder in the recent folders list, as shown above.

If it isn't there, click "Browse"

Scroll down the left hand side until you see "OneDrive". Click "OneDrive"

Word will ask you what you want to call the file.

Think of a meaningful name describing the work. In this case "Kevin Wilson Resume"

Click Save.

This will save directly to your OneDrive account.

Printing Documents

To print a document, click FILE on the top left of your screen.

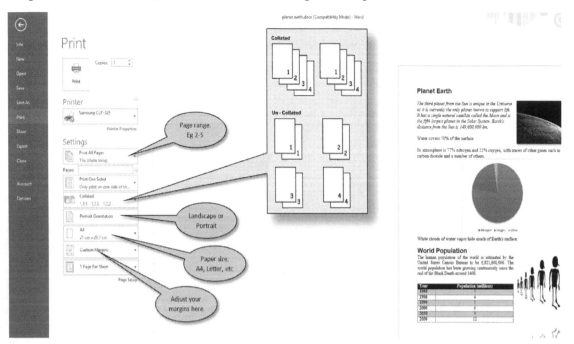

Down the left hand side you can select options such as number of copies, print individual pages instead of the whole document and adjust layout and margins.

You can adjust margins, and print pages in either landscape or portrait orientation. Portrait tends to be for documents or letters etc while landsape works well with pictures, photos etc.

Microsoft Word Mobile

Also called Word for Windows 10, this version of Microsoft Word is designed for touch screen users and allows you to create many different types of document, from letters, Resumes/CVs to greetings cards, posters and flyers all from a library of customisable templates or from scratch.

The touch screen version of Word is a cut down version of the desktop version, has a much simpler look and has the ability to save documents online using OneDrive.

Your first step in creating a document in Word is to choose whether to start from a blank document or to let a template do much of the work for you.

From then on, the basic steps in creating and sharing documents are the same.

Lets begin by launching Word

Starting Word

To launch Word go to the start screen and select "Word".

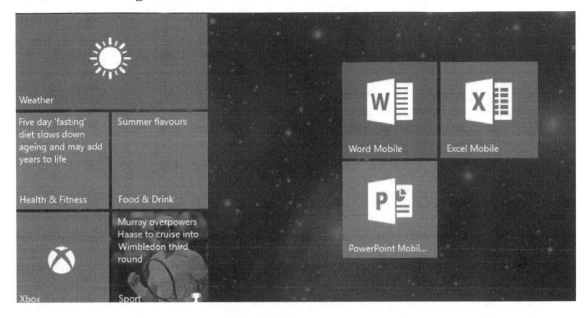

Once Word has loaded, you can select a document from a wide variety of templates, eg brochures, CVs, letters, flyers, etc. If you want to create your own just select blank. Your recently saved documents are shown on the blue pane on the left hand side.

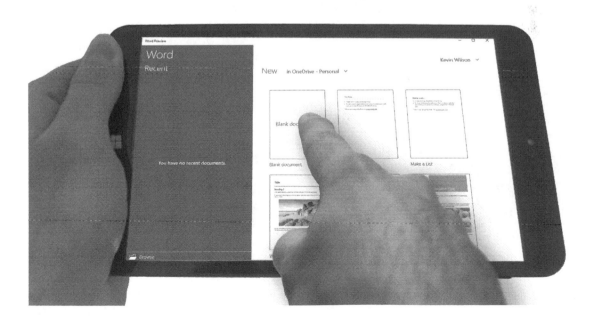

Getting Around Word

Once you select a template, you will see your main work screen.

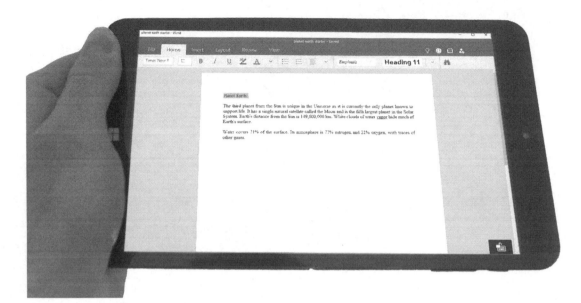

When you tap on your page an on screen keyboard will appear allowing you to enter your text.

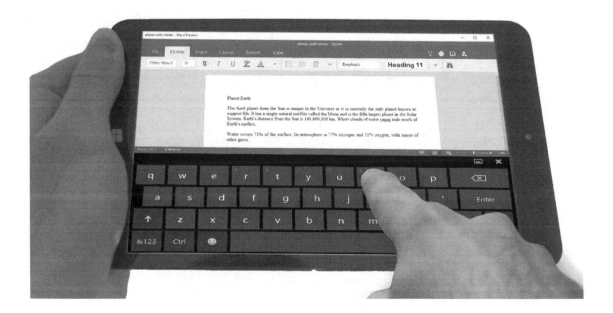

You can also plug in an external keyboard if your tablet has that ability

All the tools used in Word are organised into ribbons loosely based on their function, circled above.

Lets take a closer look.

The Home Ribbon

You will find your text formatting tools here for making text bold, changing style, font, paragraph alignment etc.

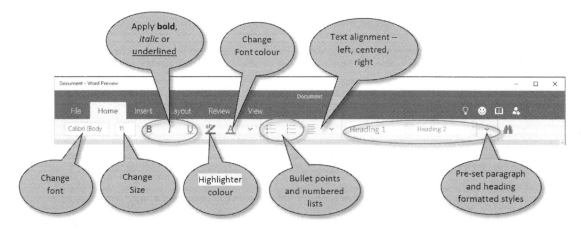

The Insert Ribbon

This is where you will find your clip-art, tables, pictures, page breaks, and pretty much anything you would want to insert into a document.

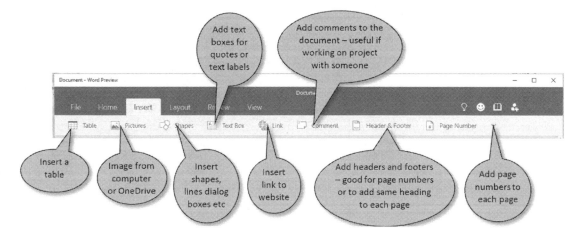

The Layout Ribbon

This ribbon you will find your page sizes, margins, page orientation (landscape or portrait) and anything to do with how your page is laid out.

The Review Ribbon

Here you can check your spelling, check and add comments. This is useful if more than one person is editing a document.

Text Formatting

To format the document we are going to use the formatting tools. These are on the home ribbon shown below.

Using Paragraph Styles

Word has a number of paragraph styles that are useful for keeping your formatting consistent.

For example you can set a font style, size and colour for a heading or title style and a different style for your text.

This makes it easier to format your document so you don't have to apply the same font style, size and colour manually every time you want to a heading.

All the styles are pre-set.

To set the styles for a heading or paragraph, just highlight it with your finger as shown below.

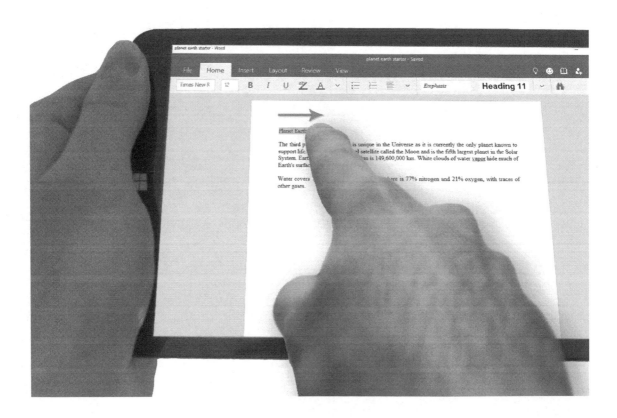

Once you have the text highlighted, click on a style from the home ribbon.

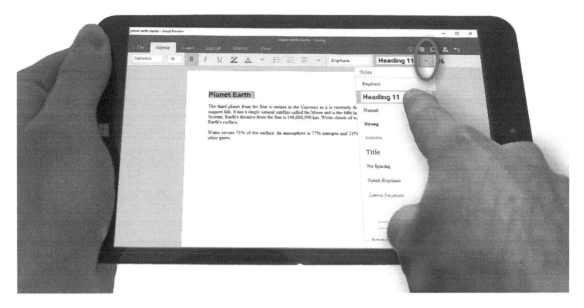

In this example I will use the title style for the heading of my document.

Bold, Italic, Underlined

You can use **bold**, *italic* or <u>underlined</u> text to emphasise certain words or paragraphs. Select the text you want to apply formatting to.

For cxample, to make the text "77% nitrogen" and "21 % oxygen" bold, select them with your finger and tap the bold icon on your home ribbon.

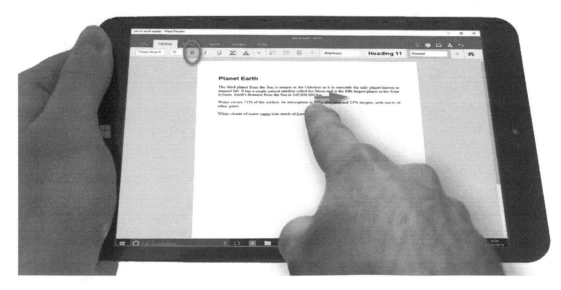

Justify Text: Left, Centred, Right, Full

You can align text to different margins.

> Most text will be **left aligned** as demonstrated in this paragraph. Only the left margin is aligned, the right margin is not.
>
> Text can also be right aligned
this is good for addresses on the top of letters
>
> Text can also be **fully justified**. This means that the left and right margins are both aligned. This helps when creating documents with images as the text will line up neatly around the image.

Select the text you want to apply formatting to.

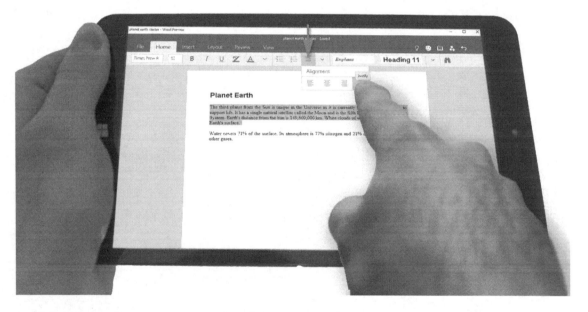

In this example, I want to make the paragraphs fully justified. This means the text is aligned both the left and right margins.

Select the text and in the home ribbon select the fully justify icon.

Cut, Copy & Paste

To ease editing documents, you can use copy, cut and paste to move paragraphs or pictures around in different parts of your document.

First select the paragraph below with your finger by tapping before the word 'white' and dragging your finger across the paragraph towards the word 'surface' in the same paragraph, as shown below. You may need to drag across the sentence then down when you get to the end of the line.

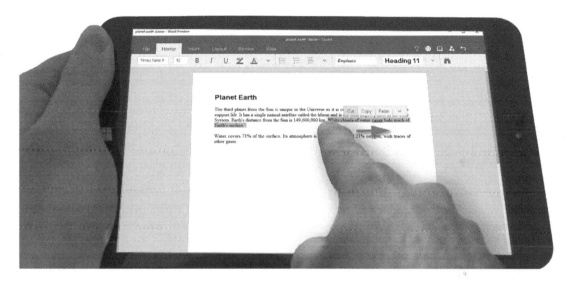

Once you have done that, tap 'cut' from the popup menu that appears.

Now tap on the position you want the paragraph you just cut out to be inserted. You may need to tap and hold your finger down for a second until the menu pops up.

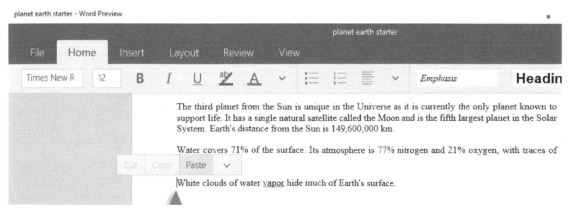

Once you have done that tap 'paste' from the popup menu. If you wanted to copy something ie make a duplicate of the text, then use the same procedure except click 'copy' instead of 'cut'.

Adding Images

You can add a photograph or picture by going to your insert ribbon and tapping on 'Pictures'

Choose the picture or photo you want from the dialog box that appears.

Tap insert.

This will insert your photo into your document. You can move the photo by clicking and dragging it to the position you want it.

You may need to resize the image, as sometimes they can come in a bit big.

To do this tap on the image, you'll see small handles appear on each corner of the image.

These are called resize handles and you can use them by tapping and dragging a corner with your finger toward the centre of the image to make it smaller as shown below.

You can also search for images on google images. When you download them, make sure you save them into your pictures folder.

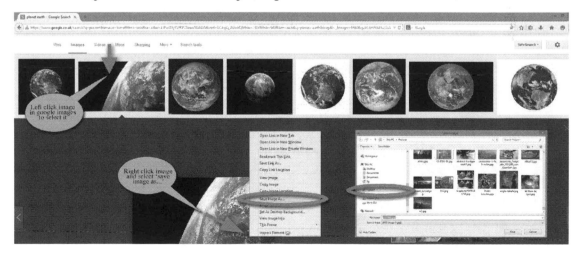

In the dialog box that appears, scroll down the left hand side and look for the pictures folder. This is sometimes under the heading 'this pc' or 'computer'.

You can add them to your document by importing them from the insert ribbon as before.

Formatting Images

When you tap on your image another ribbon appears called Picture. This allows you to add effects and layout your pictures on your page.

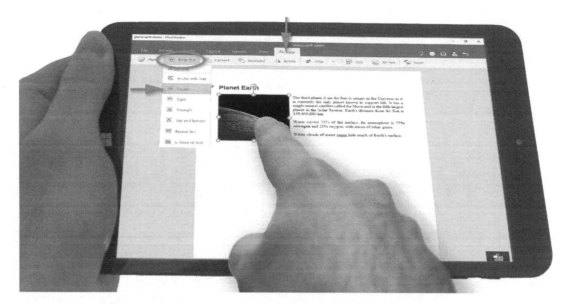

The first thing we want to do is change the text wrapping. Text wrapping enables you to surround a picture or diagram with text.

To do this, tap on your image and tap the picture ribbon.

Click Wrap Text. Then select square. This wraps the text squarely around the image.

You can now move the image into the correct position, when you do this you will find the text will wrap itself around the image.

Cropping Images

If you insert an image into your document and it has unwanted parts or you want to concentrate on one particular piece of the picture you can crop your image

First insert an image from your pictures library into your document. In this example I have used the map.

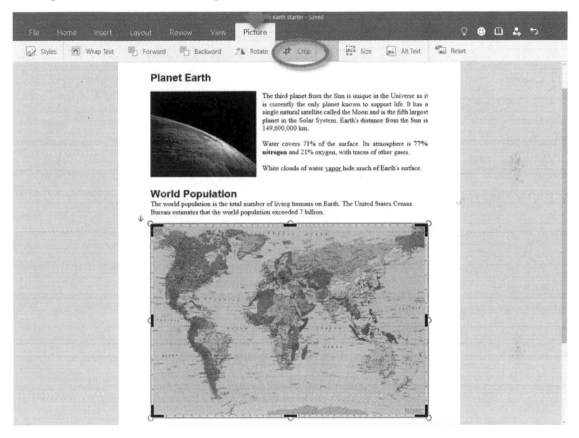

To crop the image, tap on the image then tap the picture ribbon.

From the picture ribbon tap the crop icon circled above.

If you look closely at your image you will see crop handles around the edges of the image.

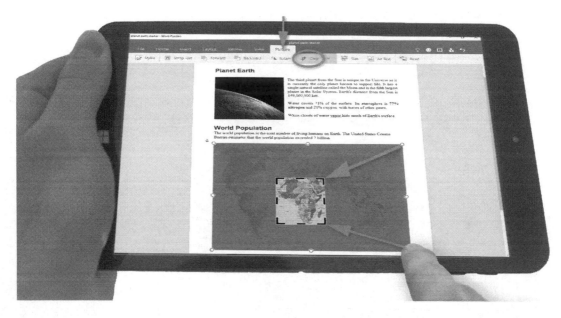

Tap and drag these around the part of the image you want as indicated by the arrows above. For example, I just want to show Africa in the map image.

The dark grey bits will be removed to leave the bit of the image inside the crop square

Adding Tables

We have added some more text about world population to our document. Now we want to add a table to illustrate our text.

To insert a table tap on your document where you want the table to appear. In this example I want it to appear just below world population paragraph.

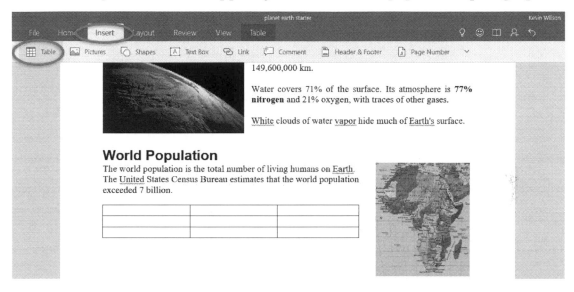

Go to your insert ribbon and tap table.

This will add a table with 1 rows & 3 columns to your document.

For this table I need four columns so we need to add another. To do this tap the table ribbon on the top right hand side

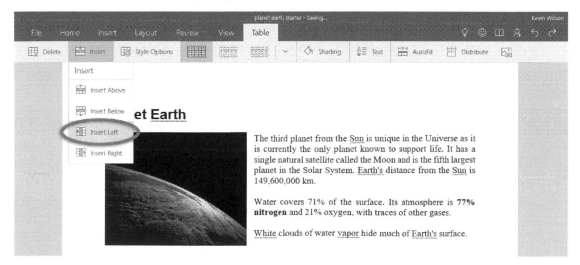

Now just fill in the table. To move between cells on the table press the tab key.

When you get to the end of the row, pressing tab will insert a new row.

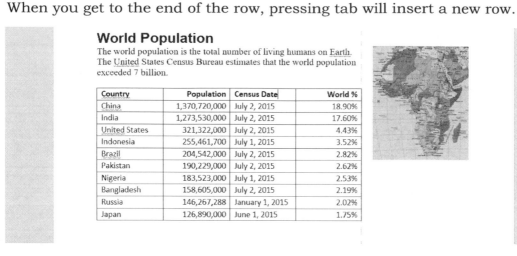

World Population

The world population is the total number of living humans on Earth. The United States Census Bureau estimates that the world population exceeded 7 billion.

Country	Population	Census Date	World %
China	1,370,720,000	July 2, 2015	18.90%
India	1,273,530,000	July 2, 2015	17.60%
United States	321,322,000	July 2, 2015	4.43%
Indonesia	255,461,700	July 1, 2015	3.52%
Brazil	204,542,000	July 2, 2015	2.82%
Pakistan	190,229,000	July 2, 2015	2.62%
Nigeria	183,523,000	July 1, 2015	2.53%
Bangladesh	158,605,000	July 2, 2015	2.19%
Russia	146,267,288	January 1, 2015	2.02%
Japan	126,890,000	June 1, 2015	1.75%

When you tap on a table, a new ribbon appears, called Table.

In the Table ribbon you have some options to shade cells, create borders etc. You can select pre designed styles by tapping on the down arrow icon on the Table ribbon circled below.

For this table I am going to choose one with shaded rows.

Templates

Microsoft Word has a wealth of pre-designed templates for you to use. You can find templates and layouts for letters, CV/Resumes, leaflets, flyers and reports

When you start Word, you will see a screen containing thumbnails of different templates that are available.

Tap on one of these thumbnails to open that template.

In the document that opens up, notice there are a number of fields. When you click on these fields they will be highlighted in grey. These are just place-holders where you can enter your information

Click on these and type in your information. You will also be able to fully edit the document as normal.

Saving Documents

Word will automatically save your documents to your OneDrive. You can rename your file by tapping on the document name at the top of the screen, then type in a name.

To force Word to save your document tap 'file', tap 'save', tap 'save copy of this file'.

Type in a file name when prompted.

Click Save.

This will save directly to your OneDrive account.

Printing Documents

To print a document, click FILE on the top left of your screen. Then tap print.

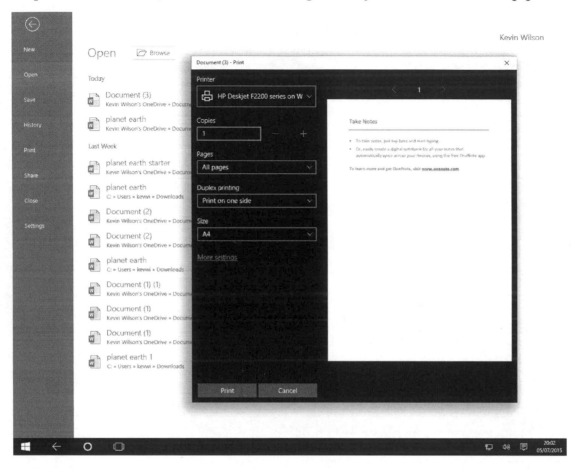

Down the left hand side in the pop up dialog box, you can select options such as number of copies, print individual pages instead of the whole document.

If you tap 'more settings', you can adjust margins, and print pages in either landscape or portrait orientation. Portrait tends to be for documents or letters etc while landsape works well with pictures, photos etc.

Chapter 6

Microsoft Power Point 2016

Microsoft PowerPoint allows you to create multimedia presentations that include animation, narration, images, and videos all from a library of pre designed templates or from a blank canvas.

PowerPoint can be used to create presentations for your up coming sales pitch. Perhaps you are giving a lecture on a specific subject or feeding back information in a meeting. All these can be enhanced using PowerPoint presentations as a visual aid.

To get your message across, you break it down into slides. Think of each slide as a canvas for the pictures, words, and shapes that will help you build your presentation.

You can also print out your presentation slides to give to your audience.

To launch PowerPoint go to the start screen and tap PowerPoint 2016

Getting Started

You can start PowerPoint 2016 by searching for it using Cortana's search field on your task bar. Type in 'powerpoint'. Then click 'PowerPoint 2016' desktop app as highlighted below.

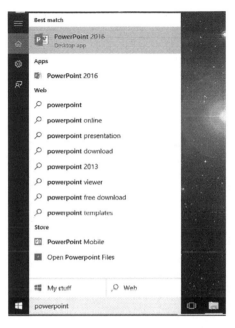

Once PowerPoint has started, select a template open a new presentation or select blank to start your own. I'm going to go with mesh template.

Your most recently saved presentations are shown on the left hand orange pane below.

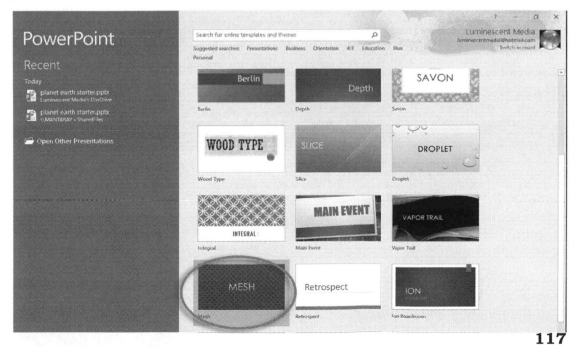

On some templates you can choose colour schemes and styles for fonts and text. The mesh template has 4 different colour schemes which affect the colour of the text. Select one and click create.

Lets take a look at PowerPoint's main screen. The tools are grouped into tabs called ribbons according to their function.

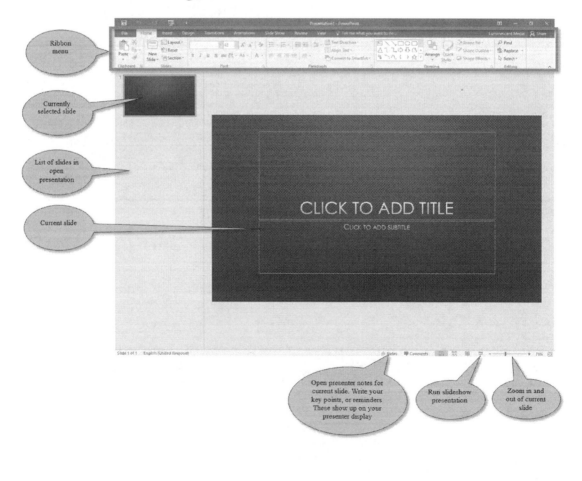

The Ribbon Menus

In PowerPoint, the tools are arranged in tabs according to their use.

Home Ribbon

All tools to do with text formatting, eg making text bold, changing fonts, and the most common tools

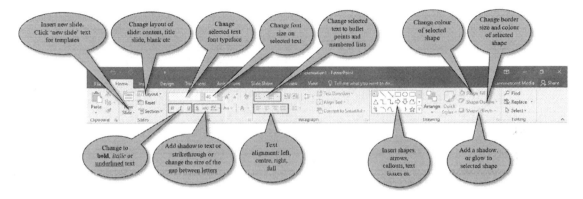

Insert Ribbon

All tools to do with inserting photos, graphics, tables, charts, sounds, movies, etc

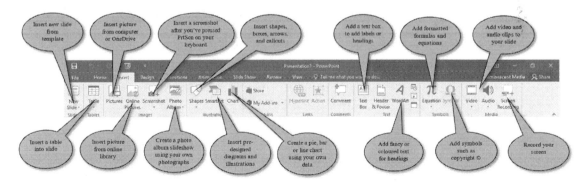

Design Ribbon

All tools to do with the look of your slide, eg, the slide background.

Transitions Ribbon

All tools to add effects to show as slides change from one to the next

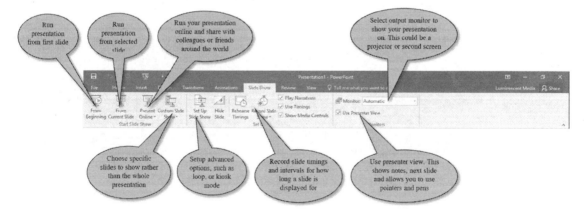

Animations Ribbon

All tools to add slide transitions and adding effects to text boxes.

Slide Show Ribbon

All tools to do with setting up your slide show and running your presentation

Designing a Slide

In PowerPoint you can add photos or clipart, charts, diagrams, text, video, sound and animations.

Lets begin by designing our slide

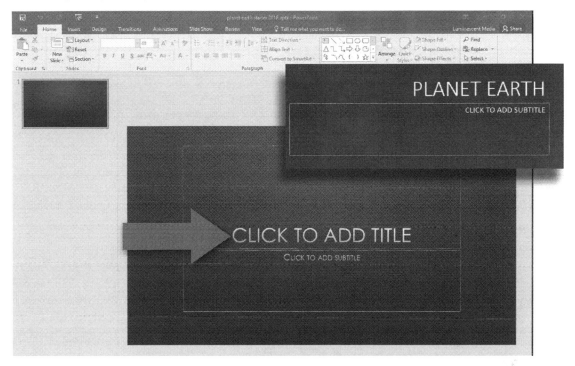

In your slide click where it says 'click to add title'. This is a place holder for you to enter your title.

Enter the title 'Planet Earth'

Add an Image

The easiest way to add an image to your slide is to first find the image in your pictures library from explorer on your desktop. The icon is on your task bar.

Open up your pictures library, then drag and drop the image onto your open slide, as shown below.

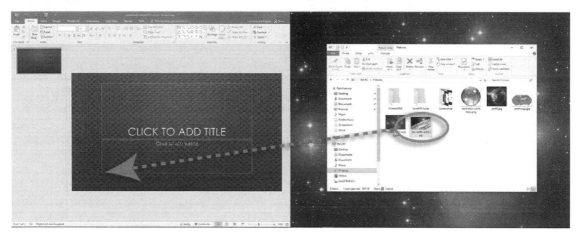

You may need to move your explorer window over to the side if it covers your PowerPoint presentation.

Resize an Images

If you click on your image you will notice a border surrounding your image.

In each corner and along the sides you will notice little squares.

These are resize handles. You can click and drag these to resize your image.

To resize the image, click and drag the resize handles until the image is the size you want.

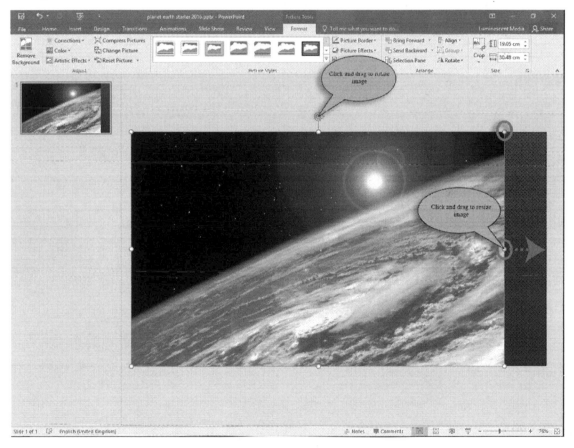

You will notice that when you have resized the image it covers the title. This is because PowerPoint constructs slides using layers. So the title "Planet Earth" will be on one layer and the image will be on another layer and because the image was inserted after the title, the image layer is on top of the title.

We can adjust this by changing the arrangement.

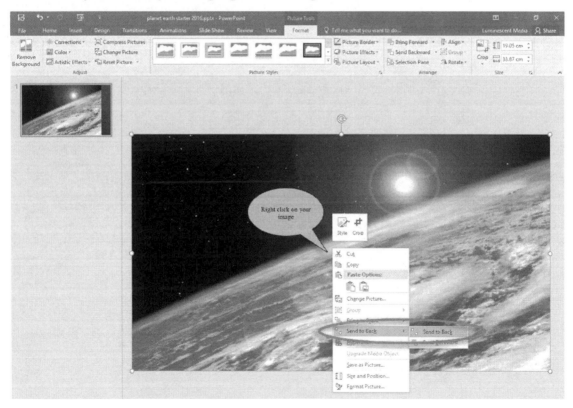

We want to put the image behind the title, so it's in the background on the slide. Right click on your image, go to 'send to back'.

From the pop down menu select 'send to back'

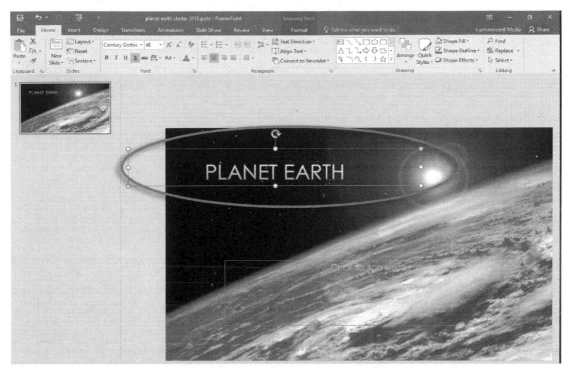

You will see the image drop behind the text layer.

This is useful if you have a lot of images and text that you need to lay out on your slide.

You can now type in the title text box 'Planet Earth' and drag it to the desired position on the slide. In my example, I'm going to put the title in the top left of the slide against the black.

Add a New Slide

To continue building our presentation we need additional slides to show our information.

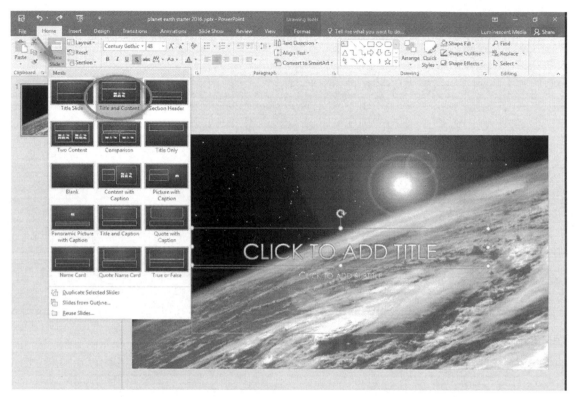

To add a new slide go to your home ribbon and click on icon 'New Slide'. Make sure you click on the text to reveal the drop down menu.

From the drop down menu select 'title and content' because we want a title on the slide but also we want to add some information in bullet points.

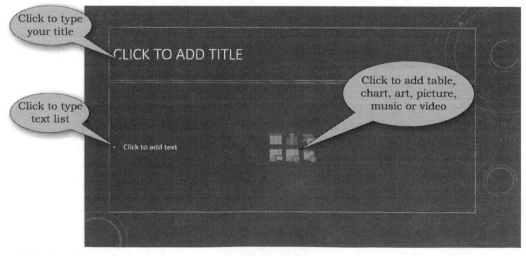

To add your text and titles just click in the text boxes and start typing your information as shown below.

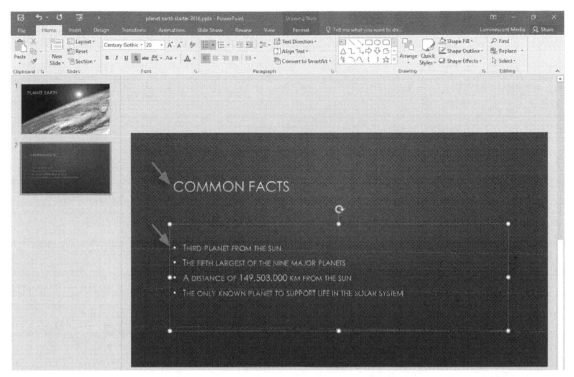

You can make text bigger by selecting it by clicking and dragging your mouse over the text so it is highlighted then click the home ribbon. From your home ribbon select the increase font size icon.

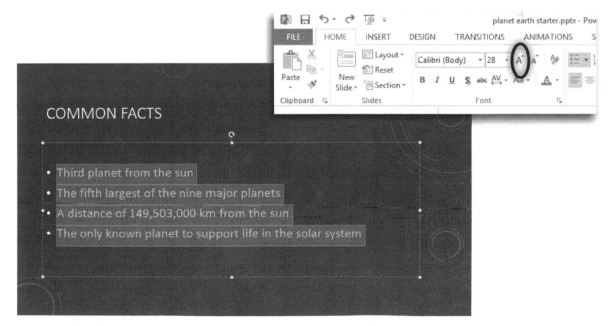

Slide Masters

Slide masters allow you to create layouts and templates that are common to all your slides, so you don't have to make those changes to each slide. A common example is, if you are creating a presentation and want a company logo on the bottom.

To edit your slide masters, go to your view ribbon and click slide master.

The larger slide listed down the left hand side is your master for all slides. The ones below are masters for specific slides such as title slides or content slides. You can split them up so you can create templates for specific slides.

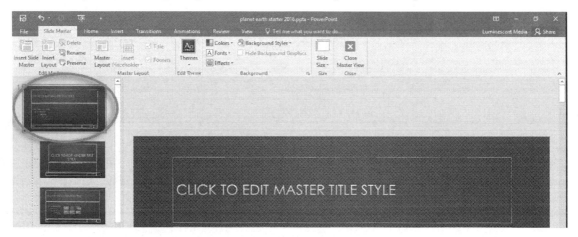

This way you can have a template for all your title slides and another one for all your content and information slides.

In this simple example, I am going to add the company logo to the bottom right of every slide.

To do this click on the larger master slide in the list on the left hand side. Open your file explorer and navigate to your images. Click and drag your image onto the master slide.

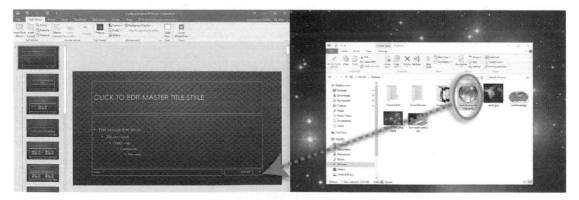

You may need to resize your image and position it in the correct place.

Insert a Table

We are going to add a table to a new slide. In this example I have added a new slide with 'title and content'

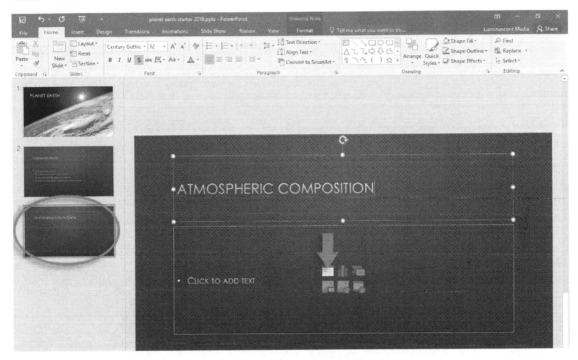

To add a table to this slide just click the table icon from the template as indicated above. In the dialog box that appears enter the number of columns and rows. This table is going to have 2 columns.

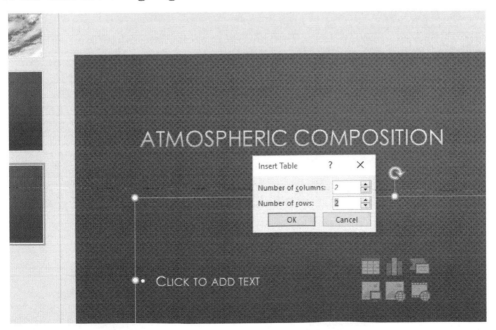

Once you have done that, enter the data into your table. Press tab key to move between cells of the table. Don't worry about the number of rows, a new row will be inserted at the end of each row when entering your data.

You can also format your table using PowerPoint's pre designed templates.

Click on the table and select the design ribbon.

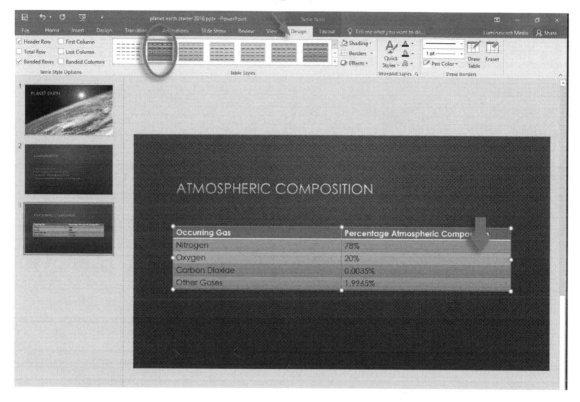

Along the centre of the design ribbon you will see a number of pre sets, you can experiment with the designs by clicking on these.

PowerPoint will automatically format the table using the colours and shadings in the templates.

Add a Chart

We are going to add a table to a new slide. In this example I have added a new slide with 'title and content'

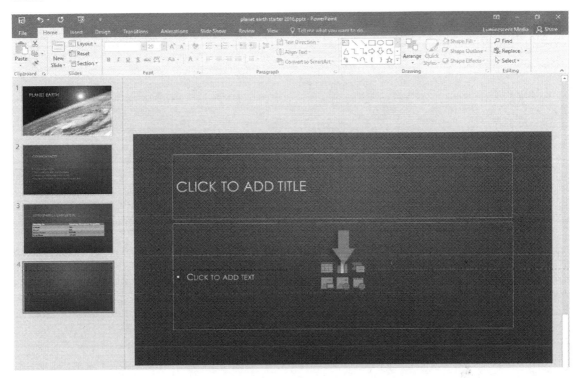

On the slide template click the chart icon shown above. From the dialog box that appears select the type of chart you want. In this example I am going to use a nice 3D pie chart.

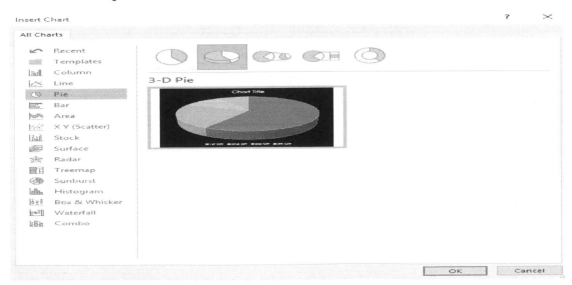

Click OK when you are done.

Enter the data in table form shown below.

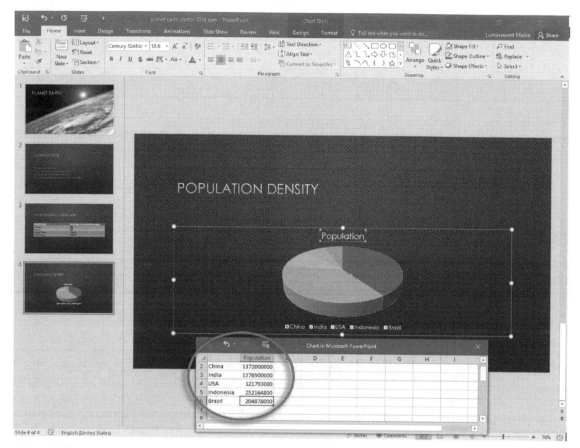

As you enter your data you'll notice PowerPoint begins to construct your chart.

Column A is the X axis on your chart, Column B is the Y axis.

Adding Special Effects

You can adjust brightness and contrast, remove backgrounds, add animations and transitions between slides.

Adjusting Images

Sometimes it helps to make some minor adjustments to your photographs or images to make them blend into your slide a little better. You can change the brightness, contrast and colours of the images. You can do all this by experimenting with the adjustments on the format ribbon.

For example. If we add another slide with the photograph of planet earth, the photo has a black background. We can make a few adjustments to this image to make it blend into the slide a little better.

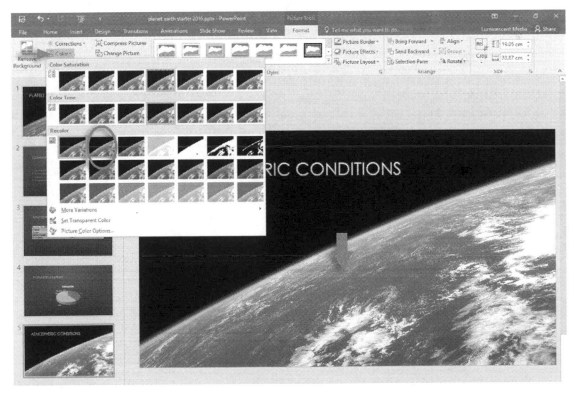

Click on the image on the slide and then click the format ribbon. On the format ribbon go to the adjustment section on the left hand side.

From the drop down menu, you can select 'color' if you want to change the colour blending of the image, eg select a blue/purple tint to match the background theme of the slide.

You can also do the same for other corrections such as brightness and contrast. Do this by selecting 'corrections' from the format ribbon instead of 'color'.

Another tip is to use the 'remove background' feature. This will only really work if the background of your image is the same colour or a plain background, such as the one below with a solid black background.

Instead of seeing the black background from the image, it would be better to use the slide background itself, rather than covering it up.

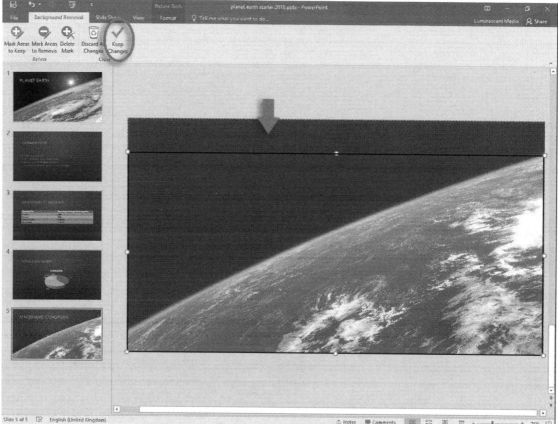

To remove the background, make sure your image is selected and click 'remove background' from the format ribbon.

This will highlight all the bits PowerPoint is going to remove from the image in dark purple. You will also notice a box surrounding the area.

Resize this box by clicking and dragging the resize handles until the box surrounds the area of the image you want to keep as shown above. In this case, around the earth.

Once you have done this click 'keep changes'

Notice you can how see the slide background instead of the black background on the image.

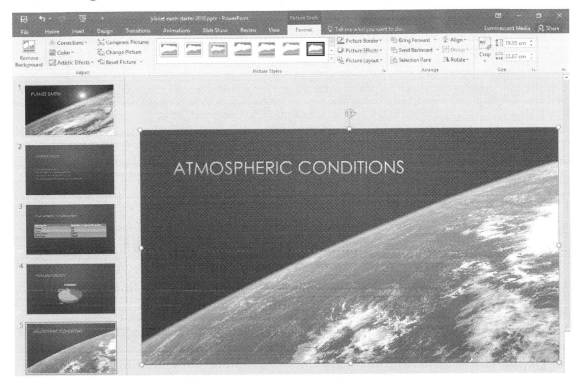

Slide Transitions

A slide transition is an animation or effect that is displayed when you move from one slide to the next.

To add transitions to PowerPoint slides click the slide you want to add the transition to then go to the transitions tab

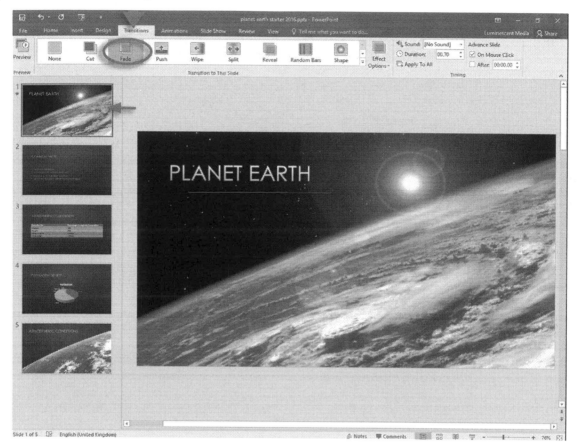

From the transitions tab you can select from a number of pre set transitions. If you click on a transition, for example 'fade', this will apply the transition to the selected slide.

To apply the transition to the whole presentation click 'apply to all', on the right hand side of the ribbon.

Slide Animations

Looking at the slide below, say you wanted each bullet point to appear one at a time instead of all at once.

You can do this by adding an animation to the text box. Click into the text box and select your animations ribbon.

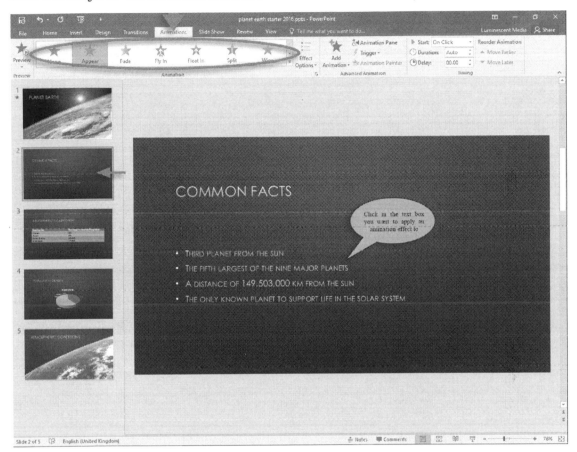

For this example, I am going to add a fade effect by selecting 'fade' from the animation pre sets circled above.

To view your presentation hit F5 on your keyboard.

Press Esc to return to PowerPoint

Print your Work

To print your document, click the File tab on the top left hand corner of the screen

In the screen below select the correct printer and number of copies you want.

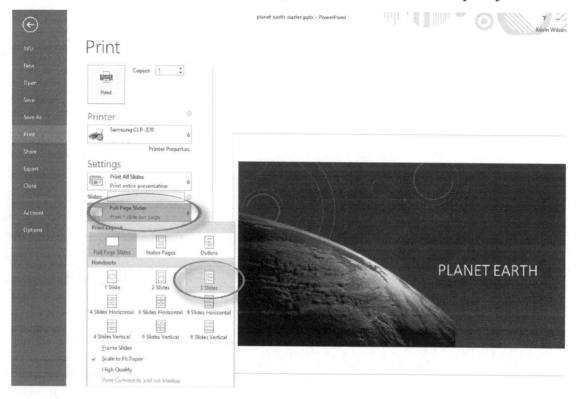

Then select how you want the presentation to print out. Click where it says "Full Page Slides".

This allows you to arrange more than one slide per page and with space to write notes.

This is useful if you are giving a copy of your slides to your audience so they can follow your presentation as you speak and take notes.

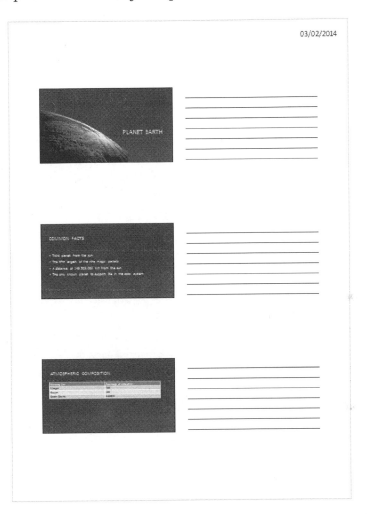

A good one is 3 slides per page with writing space next to each, shown right.

Sometimes it is useful to select 'black and white' or greyscale printing if you do not have a colour printer.

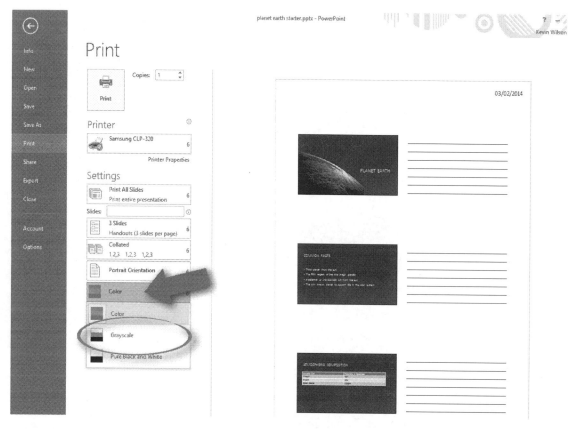

Click the print icon to print your presentation.

Microsoft Power Point Mobile

Also called Powerpoint for Windows 10, this version of Microsoft PowerPoint is designed for touch screen users and allows you to create multimedia presentations that include animation, narration, images, and videos all from a library of pre designed templates or from a blank canvas.

PowerPoint can be used to create presentations for your up coming sales pitch. Perhaps you are giving a lecture on a specific subject or feeding back information in a meeting. All these can be enhanced using PowerPoint presentations as a visual aid.

To get your message across, you break it down into slides. Think of each slide as a canvas for the pictures, words, and shapes that will help you build your presentation.

You can also print out your presentation slides to give to your audience.

To launch PowerPoint go to the start menu and tap PowerPoint

Getting Started

On your start screen click the powerpoint icon to start the application

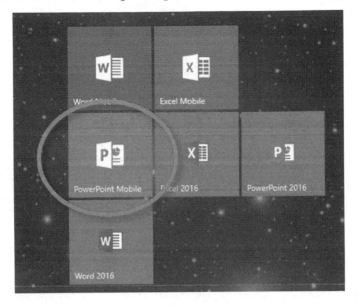

Once PowerPoint has loaded, select a template below to start a new presentation or select blank to start your own. I'm going to go with mesh template below. Your most recently saved presentations are shown on the left hand orange pane below.

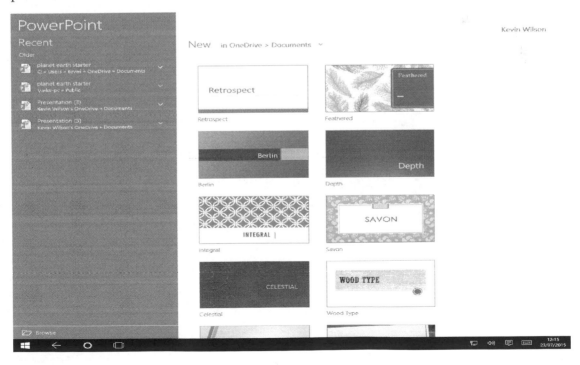

For this example, I am going to use the celestial template.

Lets take a look at PowerPoint's main screen. The tools are grouped into tabs called ribbons according to their function.

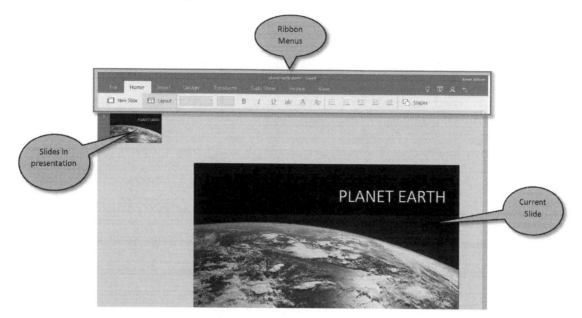

The Ribbon Menus

In PowerPoint, tools are arranged in tabs according to their use.

Home Ribbon

All tools to do with text formatting, eg making text bold, changing fonts, and the most common tools

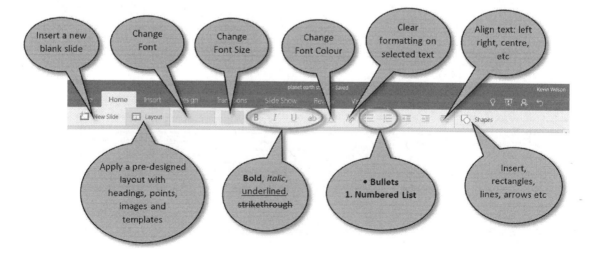

Insert Ribbon

All tools to do with inserting photos, graphics, tables, charts, sounds, movies, etc

Design Ribbon

All tools to do with the look of your slide, eg, the slide background.

Transitions Ribbon

All tools to add effects to show as slides change from one to the next

Slide Show Ribbon

All tools to do with setting up your slide show and running your presentation

Picture Ribbon

The picture ribbon appears when you tap on an image and has tools that allow you to send images behind text or infront of text if your text box happens to get covered up by a picture. You can also crop images, resize them and rotate images on an angle.

Designing a Slide

In PowerPoint you can add photos or clipart, charts, diagrams, text, video, sound and animations.

Lets begin by designing our slide

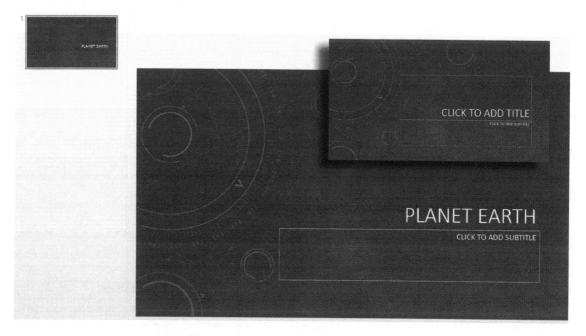

In your slide double tap where it says 'click to add title' or 'double tap to add title'. This is a place holder for you to enter your title.

Our title for the slide in this exercise is 'Planet Earth'

Add an Image

To add an image to your slide, tap the 'insert' ribbon then tap 'pictures'.

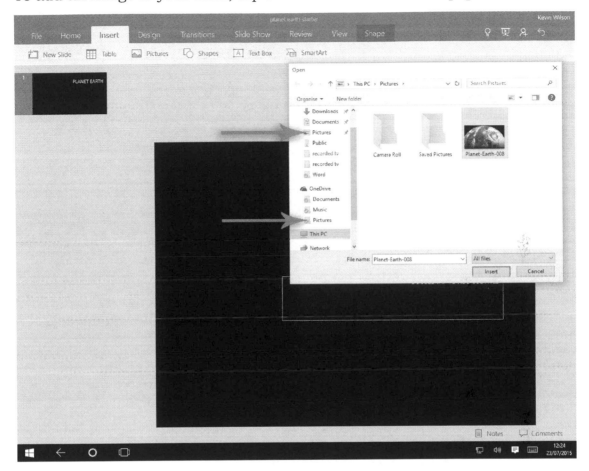

Resize an Images

If you tap on your image you will notice a border surrounding your image.

In each corner and along the sides you will notice little squares.

These are resize handles. You can tap and drag these to resize your image.

To resize the image, tap and drag the resize handles until the image is the size you want.

You will notice that when you have resized the image it covers the title. This is because PowerPoint constructs slides using layers. So the title "Planet Earth" will be on one layer and the image will be on another layer and because the image was inserted after the title, the image layer is on top of the title.

We can adjust this by changing the arrangement. Click on the image and select the picture ribbon.

From the picture ribbon tap where it says 'backward'. We want to put the image behind the title. From the drop down menu select 'send backward'

You will see the image drop behind the text layer.

If you tap on a text box such as a heading or list of bullet points, the ribbon will show as 'shape' rather than 'picture'.

This is useful if you have a lot of images and text that you need to lay out on your slide.

Add a New Slide

To continue building our presentation we need additional slides to show our information. To add a new slide go to your home ribbon and tap 'New Slide'. Make sure you click on the text to reveal the drop down menu.

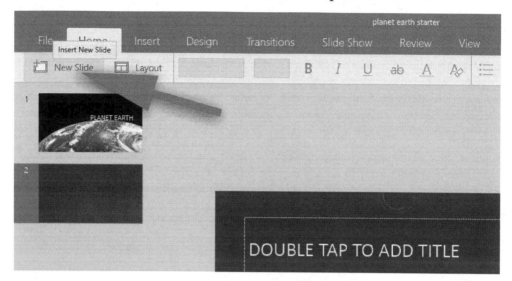

To change the layout of the slide, Tap 'layout'

From the drop down menu select 'title and content' because we want a title on the slide but also we want to add some information in bullet points.

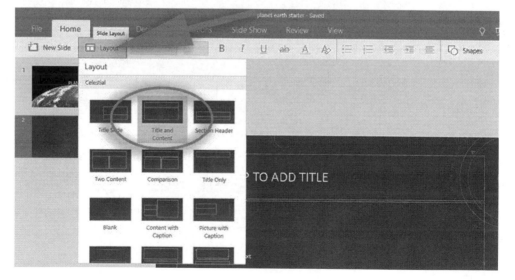

To add your text and titles just double tap in the text boxes and start typing your information as shown below.

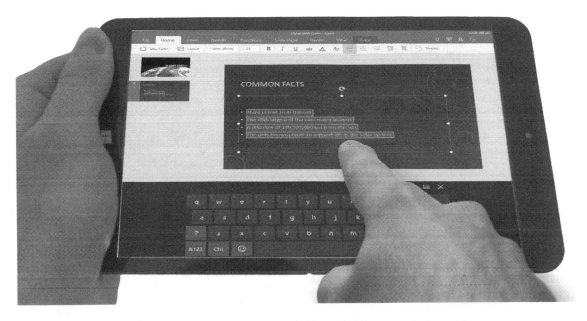

You can make text bigger by selecting it by clicking and dragging your mouse over the text so it is highlighted then click the home ribbon. From your home ribbon select the increase font size icon.

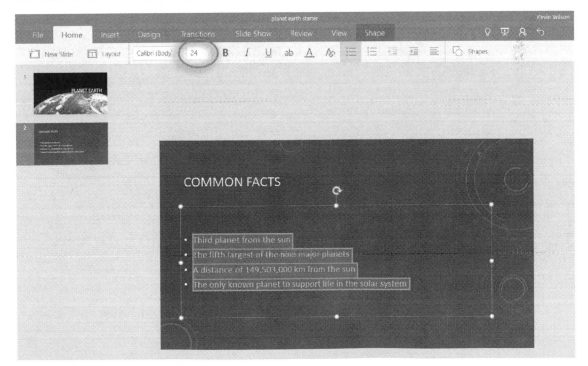

Adding Special Effects

You can adjust brightness and contrast, remove backgrounds, add animations and transitions between slides.

Slide Transitions

A slide transition is an animation or effect that is displayed when you move from one slide to the next.

To add transitions to PowerPoint slides tap the slide you want to add the transition to then go to the transitions tab

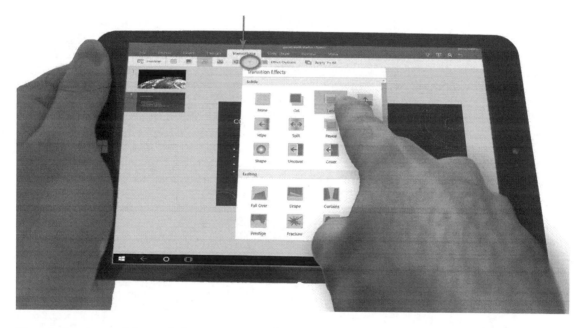

From the transitions tab you can select from a number of pre set transitions.

Tap on the downward pointing arrow circled in the screen above. This will reveal a drop down menu with a selection of transitions.

Tap on a transition. In this example I'm going to choose a fade effect.

To apply the transition to the whole presentation tap 'apply to all' once you have selected your transition.

Insert a Table

We are going to add a table to a new slide. In this example I have added a new slide with 'title and content'

To add a table to this slide tap the table icon from the 'insert ribbon'. This will automatically insert a 3x3 table (3 rows and 3 columns).

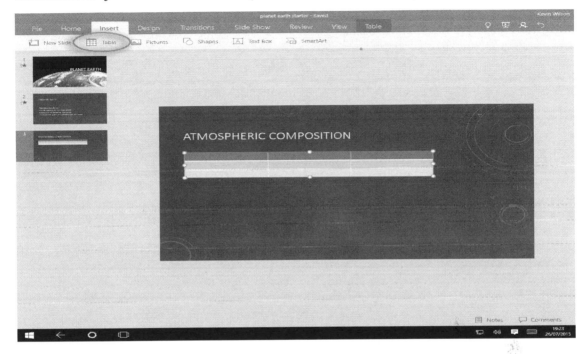

For the table in this example I only want two columns, so we need to delete one. From the 'table ribbon' that appears when you select a table, tap

Once you have done that, enter the data into your table. Press tab key to move between cells of the table.

Don't worry about the number of rows, a new row will be inserted at the end of each row when entering your data.

If you needed to insert more columns, tap insert on the 'table ribbon', and tap 'insert left' or 'insert right'.

You can resize columns if they are too small/large. To do this, tap and hold your finger on the column's dividing line, then drag it across the screen.

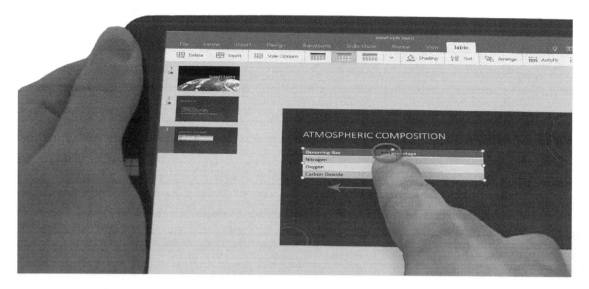

You can also format your table using PowerPoint's pre designed templates. Tap on the table in the slide and select the 'table ribbon'

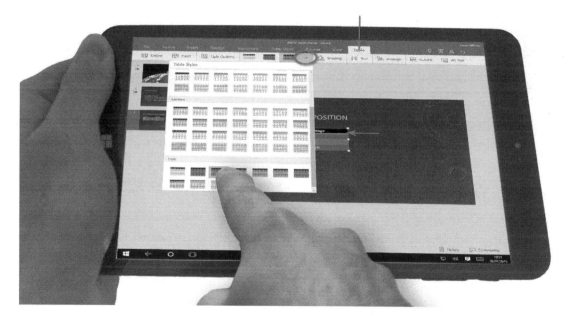

Along the centre of the table ribbon you will see a number of pre-sets, you can experiment with the designs by tapping on these. PowerPoint will automatically format the table using the colours and shadings in the templates.

Connect to a Projector

Many tablets have a micro-HDMI port (pictured right).

For example. The Surface Pro and Surface Pro 2 contain a Mini DisplayPort port (centre above). The Surface RT and Surface 2 contain a micro-HDMI port (above right).

Many modern projectors have an HDMI port (above left) so you can get cables with a micro-HDMI on one end and an HDMI on the other.

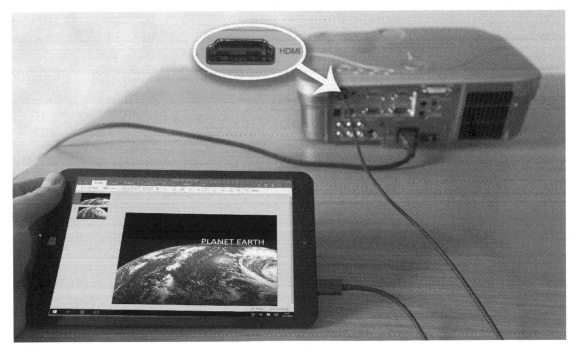

Print your Work

To print your document, click the File tab on the top left hand corner of the screen

In the screen below select the correct printer and number of copies you want.

Saving Files

Files are automatically saved to your OneDrive.

To save files, tap file, then tap save.

Select your OneDrive - Personal

Select Browse, and in the dialog box that appears, enter a name for your PowerPoint.

Chapter 8

Microsoft Excel 2016

Microsoft Excel is a spreadsheet program that allows you to store, organize, analyse and manipulate numerical data. It allows you to store and present it in tabular form or as a chart.

You can use spreadsheets to create wage slips, company accounts to analyse finance, budgets etc.

You can create simple personal budgets to keep track of your money, and create score sheets for sports events.

You can display all your data as statistical graphs and charts as well as creating tables.

To begin lets explore what a spreadsheet is.

What is a Spreadsheet?

A spreadsheet is made up of cells each identified by a reference.

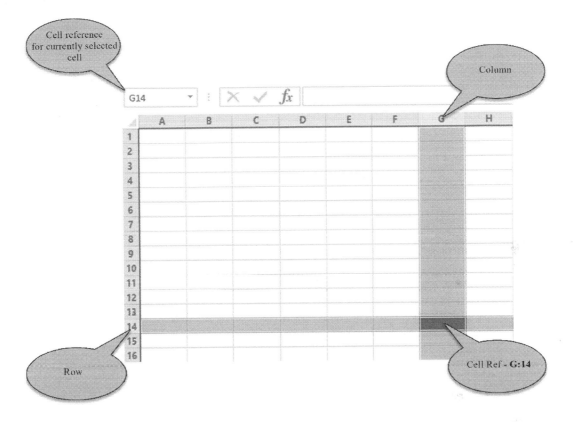

You can also select multiple cells at the same time. A group of cells is called as a cell range.

You can refer to a cell range, using the cell reference of the first cell and the last cell in the range, separated by a colon.

This cell range would be A1:D12

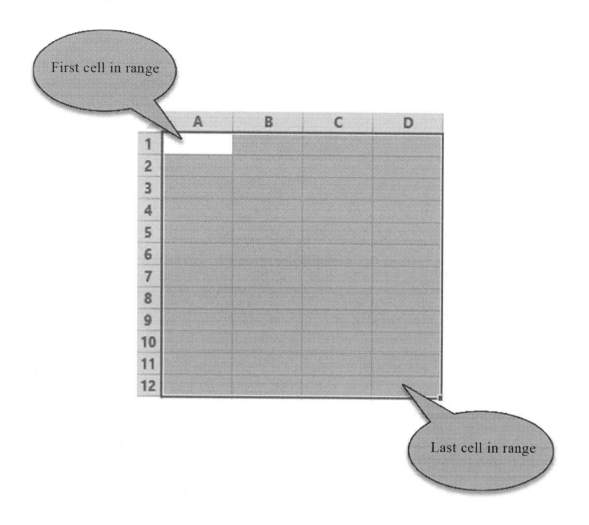

Cell references are used when you start applying formulas to the numbers in your cells.

In the example below to add two numbers you can enter a formula into cell C1.

Instead of typing in **=5+5** you would enter **=A1+B1**.

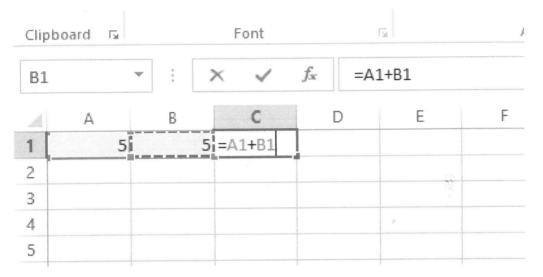

The theory is, if you enter the cell reference instead of the actual number you can perform calculations automatically and Excel will recalculate all the numbers for you should you change anything.

Eg if I wanted to change it to **5+6**, I would just change the number in cell B1 without rewriting the formula in C1.

Now you can type any number in either cell A1 or B1 and it will add them up automatically.

The Ribbon

All the tools used in Microsoft Excel are organised into ribbons loosely based on their function.

The most used ribbons are, home and formulas. For normal use of Excel these are the ones you will be looking in the most.

The Home Ribbon

This is where you will find your most used tools, basic text formatting, cell borders, cell formatting for text or numbers or currency, etc.

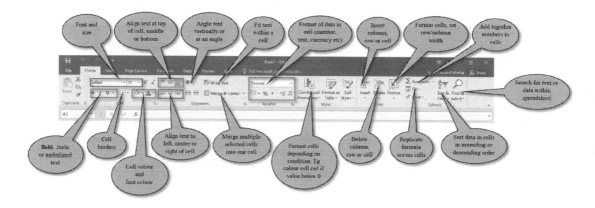

The Insert Ribbon

This is where you will find all your objects you can insert into your spreadsheet such as shapes, tables and charts.

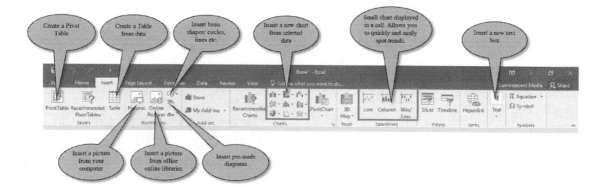

The Page Layout Ribbon

This is where you will find your page formatting functions, such as size of paper, colours & themes, paper orientation when printed, paper margins, etc.

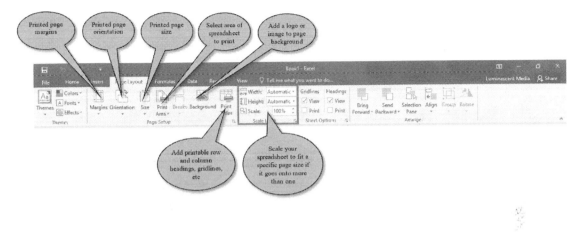

The Formulas Ribbon

This is where you will find your formulas, functions and your data manipulation tools. Sum functions, average, counting tools, etc.

The Data Ribbon

The data ribbon is where you can find tools to connect to external data sources and databases, as well as sort data.

The Review Ribbon

The review ribbon has tools that allow you to add comments as well as check spelling and protect parts of the spreadsheet from making changes.

The View Ribbon

This is where you will find your view layouts, where you can zoom into your spreadsheet etc.

Creating Spreadsheets

To begin creating your spreadsheet start typing your data into the different cells on the spreadsheet.

Entering Data

In this example we are doing a basic scoring sheet.

	A	B	C	D
1		22-Apr	29-Apr	Total
2	Barbara	21	19	
3	Ann	10	21	
4	Flo	7	7	
5	Rose	9	12	
6	Emily		0	
7	Josie	21	21	
8	Lin			
9	Joan	19		
10	Eva	21	14	
11				

Simple Text Formatting

Sometimes it improves the readability of your spreadsheet to format the data in the cells.

For example, make the heading rows bold.

You can do this by selecting the heading row as shown above and click the bold icon.

Now because the headings are quite long and take up a lot of space, you can change the orientation of the headings to read vertically instead of horizontally. This helps save space and looks better when printed on a page.

You can do this by selecting the cells you want to change the orientation. Then right click your mouse on the selection.

From the menu that appears, select 'format cells'.

In the dialog box, click the alignment tab. From there go to the orientation section on the right of the dialog box.

Click the horizontal point and drag it up to the top (the vertical point).

Or you can enter 90 in the degrees box below.

You will see the headings are now oriented vertically.

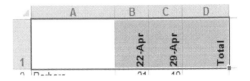

Resizing Rows and Columns

You can resize a column or row by clicking and dragging the column or row divider lines as circled below

You can also double click on these lines to automatically size the row or column to the data that is in the cell.

Inserting Rows & Columns

To insert a row between Flo and Rose, right click with your mouse on the row Rose is in. In this case row 5

From the menu click insert. This will insert a blank row above Rose.

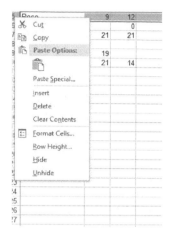

Here we can see Excel has inserted a blank row

	A	B 22-Apr	C 29-Apr	D Total
1				
2	Barbara	21	19	
3	Ann	10	21	
4	Flo	7	7	
5				
6	Rose	9	12	
7	Emily		0	
8	Josie	21	21	
9	Lin			
10	Joan	19		
11	Eva	21	14	
12				

Remember the new row or column is always inserted above or before the one selected, as shown above.

To insert a column it is exactly the same procedure except you select a column instead of a row.

	A	B 22-Apr	C 29-Apr
1		22-Apr	29-Ap
2	Barbara	21	19
3	Ann	10	21
4	Flo	7	7
5	Rose	9	12
6	Emily		0
7	Josie	21	21
8	Lin		
9	Joan	19	
10	Eva	21	14
11			
12			
13			
14			

Using Formulas

Using formulas allow you to perform calculations on the data you have entered. You can add up lists of data, multiply, subtract, find averages, plot charts all depending on what your spreadsheet is analysing.

If I wanted to add up all the scores in my score sheet, I could add another column called total and enter a formula to add up the scores for the two weeks the player has played.

To do this I need to find the cell references for Barbara's scores.

Her scores are in row 2 and columns B and C circled below.

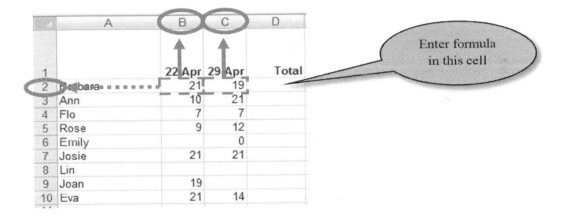

So the Cell references are B2 for her score of 21 and C2 for her score of 19.

So we enter into the cell under the heading 'total'

    = B2+C2

Remember all formulas must start with an equals sign **(=)**.

Now a little tip. To save you entering the formula for each row you can replicate it instead.

If you click on the cell D2 where you entered the formula above you will notice on the bottom right of the box is a small square handle.

I've enlarged the image so you can see it clearly.

If you click and drag this down the rest of the column you want to use the formula.

D2			✕	✓	*fx*	=C2+B2

	A	B 22-Apr	C 29-Apr	D Total
1				
2	Barbara	21	19	40
3	Ann	10	21	
4	Flo	7	7	
5	Rose	9	12	
6	Emily		0	
7	Josie	21	21	
8	Lin			
9	Joan	19		
10	Eva	21	14	
11				

Excel will automatically copy the formula and calculate the rest of the totals for you.

Using Functions

A function is a pre-defined formula. Excel has hundreds of different functions all designed to make analysing your data easier. You can find most of these functions on the formulas ribbon.

Say I wanted to add up the number of games played automatically. I could do this with a function.

Insert a new column after "29 Apr" into the spreadsheet and call it "Played". To do this right click on the D column (the 'Total' column) and from the menu click insert.

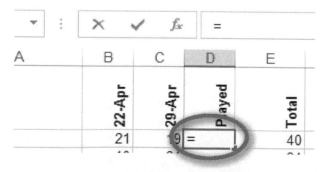

Make sure you have selected the cell you want the formula to appear in.

From the formulas ribbon click 'insert function'

In the insert function dialog box select the count function from the list, click OK

Now we need to tell the count function what we want it to count. We want to count the number of games played.

Barbara's scores are in cells B1 and C1, so highlight these two by dragging your mouse over as circled below

Click OK. You can see she has played 2 games. Now we can replicate the formula as we did before.

Click and drag the small square on the bottom right hand side of the cell.

pr	29-Apr	Played	Total
21	19	2	40
10	21		31
7	7		14
9	12		21
	0		0
21	21		42
			0
19			19
21	14		35

Drag it down down the rest of the column.

Types of Data

There are a number of different types of data you will come across using Excel. These can be numeric such as whole numbers called integers (eg 10), numbers with decimal points (eg 29.93), currencies (eg £4.67 or $43.76), as well as date and time, text and so on.

Going back to our scoring spreadsheet, we need another column for the average scores. Type the heading 'Average' as shown below.

D2	▼	⋮	✕ ✓ ƒx	=E2/D2	

◢	A	B	C	D	E	F
		22-Apr	29-Apr	Played	Total	Average
1						
2	Barbara	21	19	2	40	=E2/D2
3	Ann	10	21	2	31	
4	Flo	7	7	2	14	
5	Rose	9	12	2	21	
6	Emily		0	1	0	
7	Josie	21	21	2	42	
8	Lin			0	0	
9	Joan	19		1	19	
10	Eva	21	14	2	35	

We are going to work out the average scores over the number of games they players have played. In the Cell F2 enter the formula

```
Average = Total Score / Total number of Games Played
```

The total score is in E2 and the total number of games played is in D2.

So we enter into F2:

```
=E2 / D2
```

Use the forward slash for divide: **/**

Replicate the formula down the column as we did previously in the exercise.

Now the number format isn't as accurate as we want it. We need to tell Excel that the data in this column is a number accurate to two decimal places.

Highlight the cells you want to apply the number format to circled below.

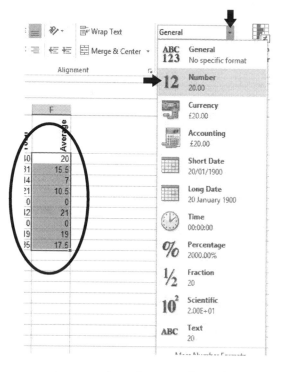

In the home ribbon go up to number format (it will currently say 'general' in box). Click the little arrow next to it.

From the drop down menu click number. This will format all the selected cells as a number with 2 decimal places.

It would be the same for if we were recording the fees paid by the players

Insert another column and call it 'fee paid'. Say the fees are 4.50. When we enter 4.5 into the column Excel thinks it's just a number, so we need to tell Excel that it is currency.

Select all the data in the fee cell.

Go back to the home ribbon and click number format.

This time select currency from the drop down menu.

This will format all the numbers as a currency.

Formatting your Spreadsheet

To emphasise certain parts of your spreadsheet such as totals or headings you can apply borders and shading to cells or groups of cells.

Cell Alignment

This helps to align your data inside your cells and make it easier to read.

To do this highlight the cells you want to apply the alignment to, then select 'centre' from the alignment icons highlighted above. The top three align vertically in the cell, the bottom three align horizontally in the cell.

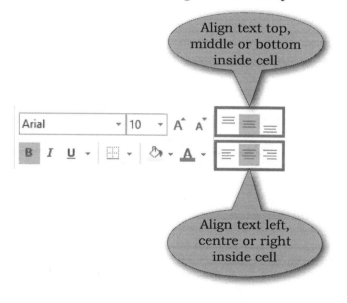

Text Format

As well as aligning the text inside your cell, you can apply bold or italic effects to make certain parts such as headings stand out.

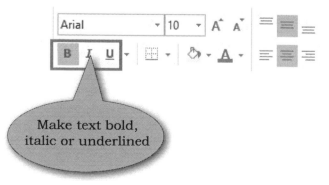

You can also change the font and size.

To do this in our spreadsheet highlight the headings ('22-Apr' to 'Fee Paid') and then click the bold icon highlighted below.

To align your text in the cells in the centre, again select the cells you want then click the centre icon as highlighted below.

Cell Borders

To apply borders to your spreadsheet. Select with your mouse the cells you want to format. In this case I am going to do the whole table.

Right click on the selected cells and select 'format cells' from the menu.

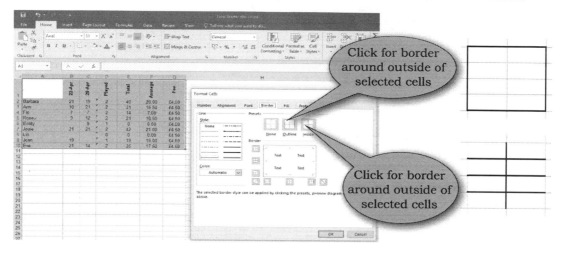

I want the borders around all the cells both inside and the outline. So from the dialog box click 'outline' & 'inside'.

Now you can tweak the borders around individual cells. For example, it would make our spreadsheet easier to read if we separated the names from the scores and from the totals. We can do this by adding borders to the cells.

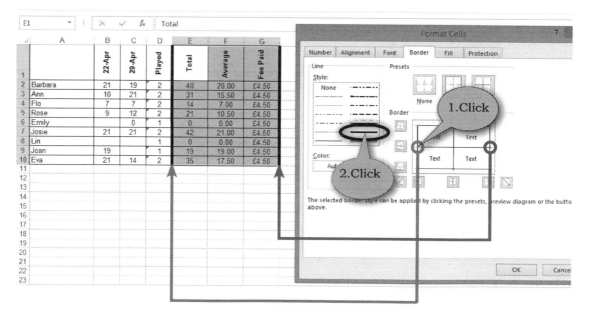

In the dialog box select the left most line under the border section. Then under the style section select the size of your line circled above.

Do this with the '22-Apr' column too.

First, highlight the column as shown below. Right click on selection and select 'format cells' from the menu...

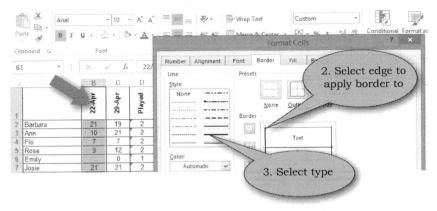

Select the edge that corresponds to the edge of the cell under the border secion in the dialog box. Then select the style of your line, eg dotted line, solid line, thick line etc.

Adding a Chart

The easiest way to add a chart is to select from your spreadsheet a column you want for the X-Axis and a column you want for the Y-Axis.

I am going to do a chart on the total scores.

First select all the names in the first column. This will be the X-Axis on the chart.

	A	B	C	D	E	F	G
1		22-Apr	29-Apr	Played	Total	Average	Fee
2	Barbara	21	19	2	40	20.00	£9.00
3	Ann	10	21	2	31	15.50	£9.00
4	Flo	7	7	2	14	7.00	£9.00
5	Rose	9	12	2	21	10.50	£9.00
6	Emily		0	1	0	0.00	£9.00
7	Josie	21	21	2	42	21.00	£9.00
8	Lin			0	0	#DIV/0!	£9.00
9	Joan	19		1	19	19.00	£9.00
10	Eva	21	14	2	35	17.50	£9.00
11							
12							
13							

(Name box shows: 10R x 1C)

Now hold down the control key on your keyboard. This allows you to multi-select.

While holding control, select the data in the total column with your mouse.

This will be the Y-Axis on the chart. Note the data in the names column is still highlighted

	A	B	C	D	E	F	G
1		22-Apr	29-Apr	Played	Total	Average	Fee
2	Barbara	21	19	2	40	20.00	£9.00
3	Ann	10	21	2	31	15.50	£9.00
4	Flo	7	7	2	14	7.00	£9.00
5	Rose	9	12	2	21	10.50	£9.00
6	Emily		0	1	0	0.00	£9.00
7	Josie	21	21	2	42	21.00	£9.00
8	Lin			0	0	#DIV/0!	£9.00
9	Joan	19		1	19	19.00	£9.00
10	Eva	21	14	2	35	17.50	£9.00
11							
12							
13							

(Name box shows: E1, formula bar shows: Total)

Release the control key and go to the insert ribbon.

In the centre of the ribbon you will find some different types of charts – line charts, column charts, pie charts.

I am going for a nice 3D column chart.

Click the column chart icon, circled below, to add the chart.

You are automatically taken to the design ribbon where you can select a style to auto-format the chart for you.

Select a style from the options, that looks good. I'm going for a nice shaded effect that matches my shading on my table.

Printing your Spreadsheet

To print your document, click 'file' on the top left hand corner of the screen

In the menu down the left hand side select print.

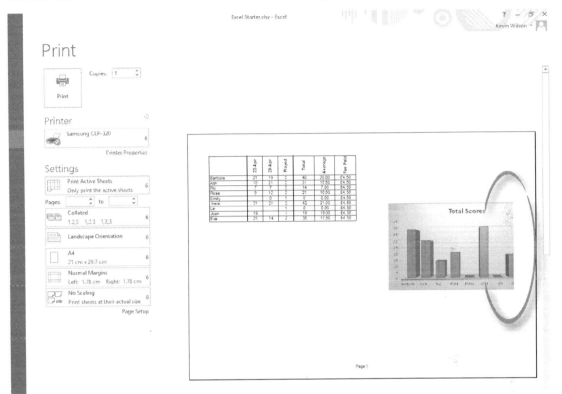

From here you can select the number of copies, the printer you're using, the range or pages you want to print. For example, if you just want to print the first page, last page etc. You can select landscape or portrait paper orientation - use landscape for printing spreadsheets. Paper size such as letter or A4, and margins, you can adjust from here. Scaling can be used to make the spreadsheet bigger or smaller to fit your page.

A tip when printing in Excel is to keep an eye on the preview you can see on the right hand side of the screen above. Notice how the chart is cut off. Sometimes columns can be cut off too.

You can adjust this by going back to your spreadsheet. Do this by clicking the back arrow on the very top left of the screen.

This will take you back to your spreadsheet.

Excel will have placed dotted lines showing the edge of the page print area. Move the content you want on the page inside this area, either by moving charts by dragging or resizing columns etc.

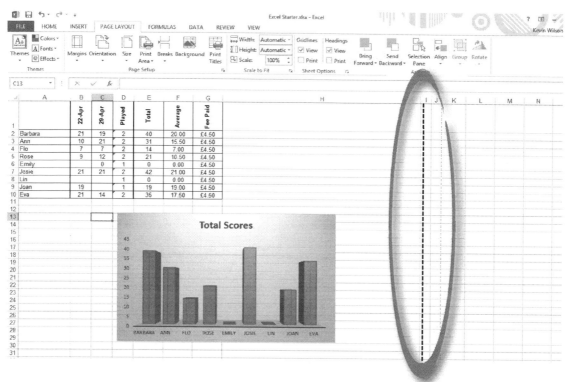

Also check your margins on the page layout ribbon, select narrow.

Now go to print your spreadsheet as before. (File -> Print)

Once you are happy with the print preview, print your document.

Click the print icon to send the spreadsheet to the printer.

Saving Files

To save files, click the small disk icon in the top left hand corner of your screen

Select your OneDrive - Personal

Select Browse, and in the dialog box that appears, enter a name for your spreadsheet.

Chapter

9

Microsoft Excel Mobile

Also called Excel for Windows 10, this version of Microsoft Excel is designed for touch screen users and allows you to store, organize, analyse and manipulate numerical data with a flick of a finger. It allows you to store and present it in tabular form or as a chart.

You can use spreadsheets to create wage slips, company accounts to analyse finance, budgets etc.

You can create simple personal budgets to keep track of your money, and create score sheets for sports events.

You can display all your data as statistical graphs and charts as well as creating tables.

To begin lets explore what a spreadsheet is.

Getting Started

Start excel by tapping on the icon on your start screen.

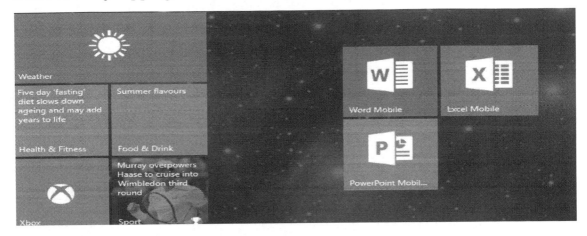

Tap on a blank workbook.

The Ribbon

All the tools used in Microsoft excel are organised into ribbons loosely based on their function.

The most used ribbons are, home and formulas. For normal use of excel these are the ones you will be looking in the most.

The Home Ribbon

This is where you will find your most used tools, basic text formatting, cell borders, cell formatting for text or numbers or currency, etc.

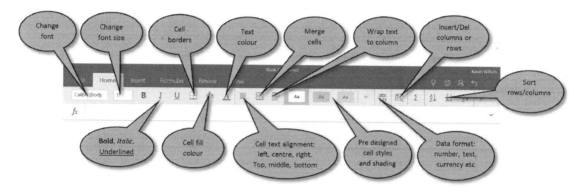

The Insert Ribbon

This is where you will find all your objects you can insert into your spreadsheet such as shapes, tables and charts.

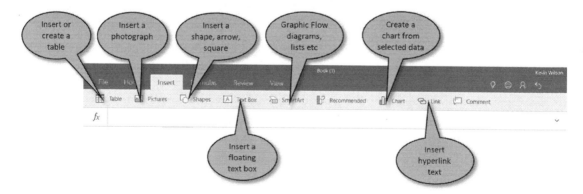

The Formulas Ribbon

This is where you will find your formulas, functions and your data manipulation tools. Sum functions, average, counting tools, etc.

The Review Ribbon

This is where you will find tools to add comments to your excel spreadsheet. This is useful if more than one person is working on a large spreadsheet.

The View Ribbon

From this ribbon you can show or hide the formula bar, spreadsheet gridlines, column and row headings as well as the tabs along the bottom of your spreadsheet (sheet1, sheet2, sheet3 and so on).

Creating Spreadsheets

To begin creating your spreadsheet start typing your data into the different cells on the spreadsheet.

Entering Data

In this example we are doing a basic scoring sheet.

	A	B	C	D
1		22-Apr	29-Apr	Total
2	Barbara	21	19	
3	Ann	10	21	
4	Flo	7	7	
5	Rose	9	12	
6	Emily		0	
7	Josie	21	21	
8	Lin			
9	Joan	19		
10	Eva	21	14	
11				

You can do this by selecting the heading row as shown above and click the bold icon.

Resizing Rows and Columns

You can resize a column or row by tapping and dragging the column or row divider lines as circled below

You can also double tap on these lines to automatically size the row or column to the data that is in the cell.

Inserting Rows & Columns

To insert a row between Flo and Rose, tap on the row Rose is in. In this case row 5.

From the home ribbon tap the cells icon. This will insert a blank row above Rose.

To insert a column it is exactly the same procedure except you select a column instead of a row.

Remember the new row or column is always inserted above or before the one selected, as shown above.

Using Formulas

Using formulas allow you to perform calculations on the data you have entered. You can add up lists of data, multiply, subtract, find averages, plot charts all depending on what your spreadsheet is analysing.

If I wanted to add up all the scores in my score sheet, I could add another column called total and enter a formula to add up the scores for the two weeks the player has played.

To do this I need to find the cell references for Barbara's scores.

Her scores are in row 2 and columns B and C circled below.

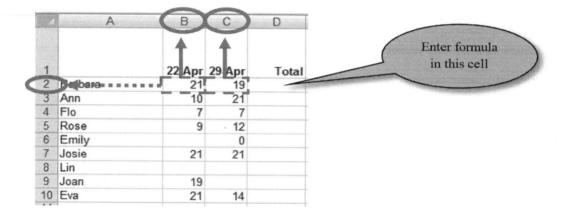

So the Cell references are B2 for her score of 21 and C2 for her score of 19.

So we enter into the cell under the heading 'total'

    = B2+C2

Remember all formulas must start with an equals sign (=).

Copying Formulas

Instead of typing in the same formula for every row you can copy and paste formulas.

To do this tap and hold your finger on the cell you want to copy until the menu appears.

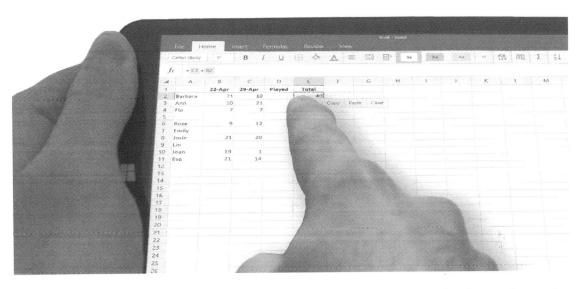

From the menu tap 'copy'. In this example, I want to copy the formula to the other cells in the 'total' column.

Tap and hold your finger on the glass on the first cell you want to formula in. Then drag down the column of cells you want to copy the formula to.

Hold your finger on the last cell until the menu appears.

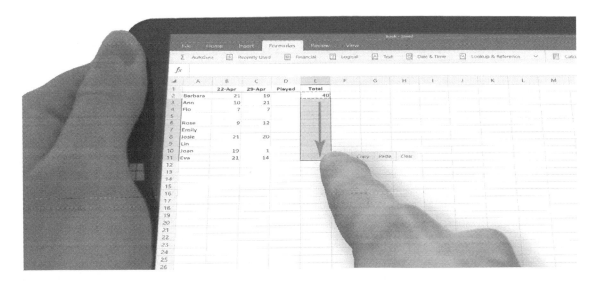

From the menu, tap 'paste'

Using Functions

A function is a pre-defined formula. Excel has hundreds of different functions all designed to make analysing your data easier. You can find most of these functions on the formulas ribbon.

Say I wanted to add up the number of games played automatically. I could do this with a function.

Insert a new column after "29 Apr" into the spreadsheet and call it "Played".

To do this right click on the D column (the 'Total' column) and from the home ribbon tap the cells icon then tap insert columns from the drop down menu.

Make sure you have selected the cell you want the formula to appear in.

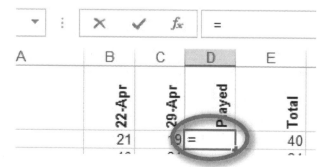

From the formulas ribbon tap 'fx'

From the drop down menu select 'count'. If it isn't there, you can either tap on the categories listed down the menu or type in the function name using the pop up keyboard (tap the icon bottom right of screen)

Now we need to tell the count function what we want it to count. We want to count the number of games played.

Barbara's scores are in cells B1 and C1, so highlight these two by dragging your finger over as shown below

Now we can replicate the formula as we did before.

Types of Data

There are a number of different types of data you will come across using Excel. These can be numeric such as whole numbers called integers (eg 10), numbers with decimal points (eg 29.93), currencies (eg £4.67 or $43.76), as well as date and time, text and so on.

Going back to our scoring spreadsheet, we need another column for the average scores. Type the heading 'Average' as shown below.

| D2 ▾ | ⋮ | ✕ ✓ *fx* | =E2/D2 |

◢	A	B 22-Apr	C 29-Apr	D Played	E Total	F Average
1						
2	Barbara	21	19	2	40	=E2/D2
3	Ann	10	21	2	31	
4	Flo	7	7	2	14	
5	Rose	9	12	2	21	
6	Emily		0	1	0	
7	Josie	21	21	2	42	
8	Lin			0	0	
9	Joan	19		1	19	
10	Eva	21	14	2	35	

We are going to work out the average scores over the number of games they players have played. In the Cell F2 enter the formula

```
Average = Total Score / Total number of Games Played
```

The total score is in E2 and the total number of games played is in D2.

So we enter into F2:

```
=E2 / D2
```

Use the forward slash for divide: **/**

Replicate the formula down the column as we did previously in the exercise.

Now the number format isn't as accurate as we want it. We need to tell excel that the data in this column is a number accurate to two decimal places.

Highlight the cells you want to apply the number format to circled below.

In the home ribbon go up to number format (abc123). Tap 'number'.

It would be the same for if we were recording the fees paid by the players

Insert another column and call it 'fee paid'. Say the fees are 4.50.

When we enter 5.0 into the column excel thinks it's just a number, so we need to tell excel that it is currency.

Select all the data in the 'fee' cell.

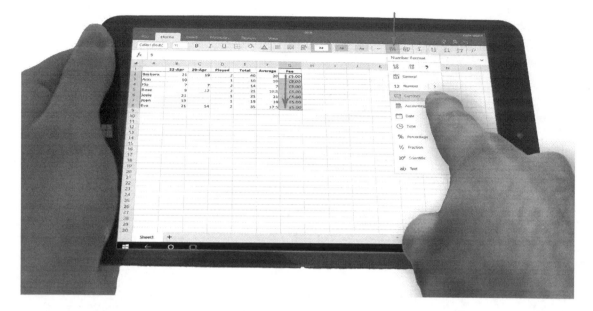

Go back to the home ribbon and tap number format (abc123).

This time select currency from the drop down menu.

This will format all the numbers as a currency (£ or $).

Adding a Chart

The easiest way to add a chart is to select from your spreadsheet a column you want for the X-Axis and a column you want for the Y-Axis.

I am going to do a chart on the total scores.

First select the whole table. Tap and hold your finger on the first cell then drag the box across all the cells in the table.

From the Insert Ribbon, tap 'Chart'. In the drop down menu you will find some different types of charts – line charts, column charts, pie charts.

I am going for a nice column chart. To do this tap 'Column'

Tap on a chart to add to your spreadsheet.

Now here is the tricky bit. You will notice that the chart wizard has added all the columns to the chart which isn't very informative.

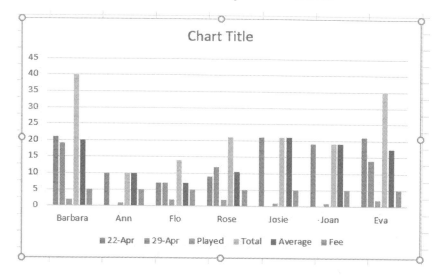

In this example, I only want column A (name) and column E (total) to show in the chart.

You will notice green dots you can use to select the column you want to show.

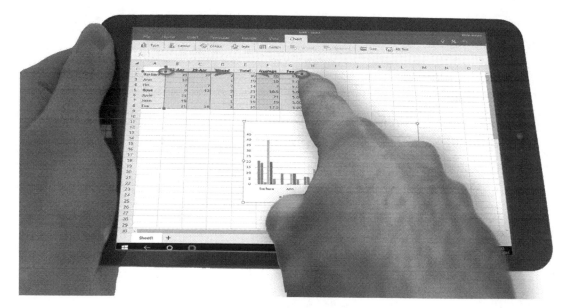

Drag these dots to the column you want for the Y axis of your chart. In this case, the 'total' column.

The X Axis is column A

The Y Axis you can select by moving the green dots as shown above.

Formatting your Spreadsheet

To emphasise certain parts of your spreadsheet such as totals or headings you can apply borders and shading to cells or groups of cells.

Cell Alignment

This helps to align your data inside your cells and make it easier to read.

To do this, highlight the cells you want to align, then from the home ribbon, tap the cell alignment icon.

Select 'centre' from the alignment icons highlighted above. The top three align vertically in the cell, the bottom three align horizontally in the cell.

Text Format

As well as aligning the text inside your cell, you can apply bold or italic effects to make certain parts such as headings stand out.

You can also change the font and size.

To do this in our spreadsheet highlight the headings ('22-Apr' to 'Fee Paid') and then click the bold icon highlighted above.

To align your text in the cells in the centre, again select the cells you want then click the centre icon as highlighted in top image.

Cell Borders

To apply borders to your spreadsheet. Select the cells you want to format. In this case I am going to do the whole table.

I want the borders around all the cells both inside and the outline. Tap 'outline' & 'inside' (circled above).

Now you can tweak the borders around individual cells. For example, it would make our spreadsheet easier to read if we separated the names from the scores and from the totals. We can do this by adding borders to the cells.

Printing your Spreadsheet

To print your document, tap 'file' on the top left hand corner of the screen

In the menu down the left hand side select print.

From here you can select the number of copies, the printer you're using, the range or pages you want to print. For example, if you just want to print the first page, last page etc. You can select landscape or portrait paper orientation - use landscape for printing spreadsheets. Paper size such as letter or A4, and margins, you can adjust from here. Scaling can be used to make the spreadsheet bigger or smaller to fit your page.

A tip when printing in excel is to keep an eye on the preview you can see on the right hand side of the screen above. Notice how the chart is cut off. Sometimes columns can be cut off too.

You can adjust this by going back to your spreadsheet. Do this by clicking the back arrow on the very top left of the screen.

This will take you back to your spreadsheet.

Excel will have placed dotted lines showing the edge of the page print area. Move the content you want on the page inside this area, either by moving charts by dragging or resizing columns etc.

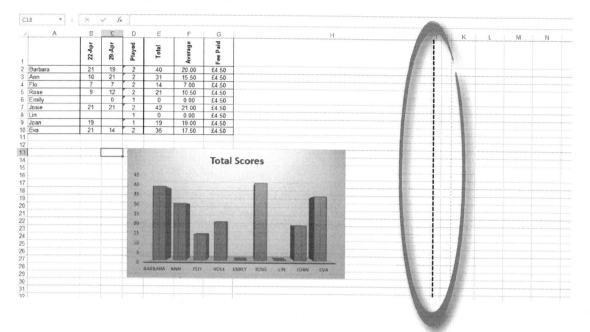

Now go to print your spreadsheet as before. (File -> Print)

Once you are happy with the print preview, print your document.

Saving Files

Files are automatically saved to your OneDrive.

To save files, tap file, then tap save.

Select your OneDrive - Personal

Select Browse, and in the dialog box that appears, enter a name for your spreadsheet.

Chapter 10

Microsoft Access 2016

Microsoft Access 2016 is a database creation and management program and allows you to manage and store information for the purpose of reporting and analysis.

You can store names and addresses of people you write to and quickly generate mail shots using mail merge.

If you run a business you can store all your suppliers, customers, orders, invoices etc and generate these as you service your customers or order new stock.

If you ever visit the doctor, your details are stored in a database.

These are just a few examples of databases.

To understand Access, you must first understand databases.

What is a Database

A database is a collection of records stored in a computer system. A storage and retrieval system that allows users to enter, access, and analyse data quickly and easily.

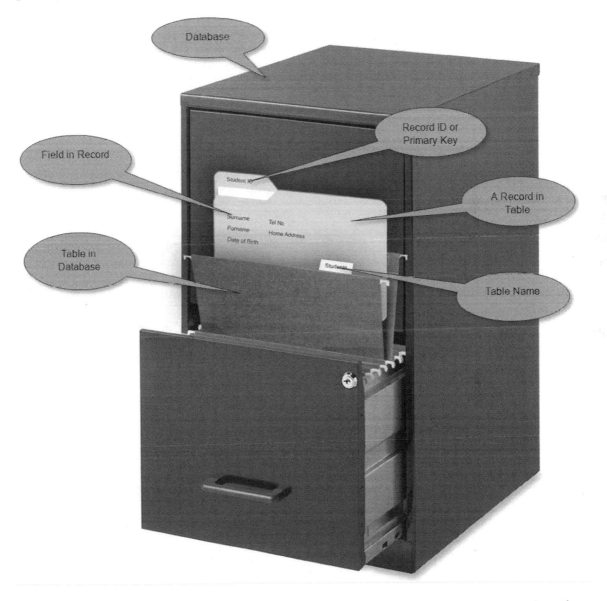

Databases can store information on almost anything. There are national databases that store driver and car registrations, details on individuals.

Microsoft Access Databases

In Access, every database is stored in a single file that contains database objects

Tables store information using individual fields. A field is just a piece of information such as name or date of birth. This is where you start to build your database, using tables to store your information.

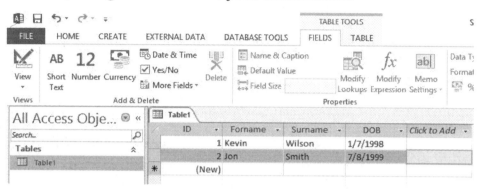

Queries let you retrieve information. Or query the database. Depending on what your database stores, you can create queries to return a list of students in a particular year, or best selling items and so on.

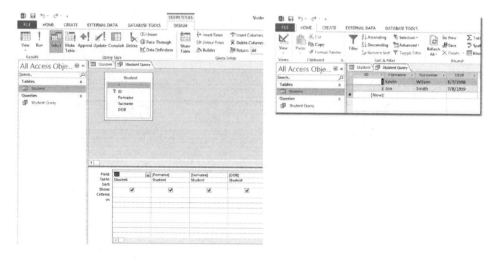

Forms provide the user interface of the database and allow you to create arrange, and colourize the fields from your tables into an easy way for users to interact with the database.

Forms provide an easy way to view or change the information in a table in a more user friendly fashion.

Reports allow you print information from a table or query. You can format the information into easily readable reports direct from your tables or more commonly from a query. Eg a list of the students in a particular class or year.

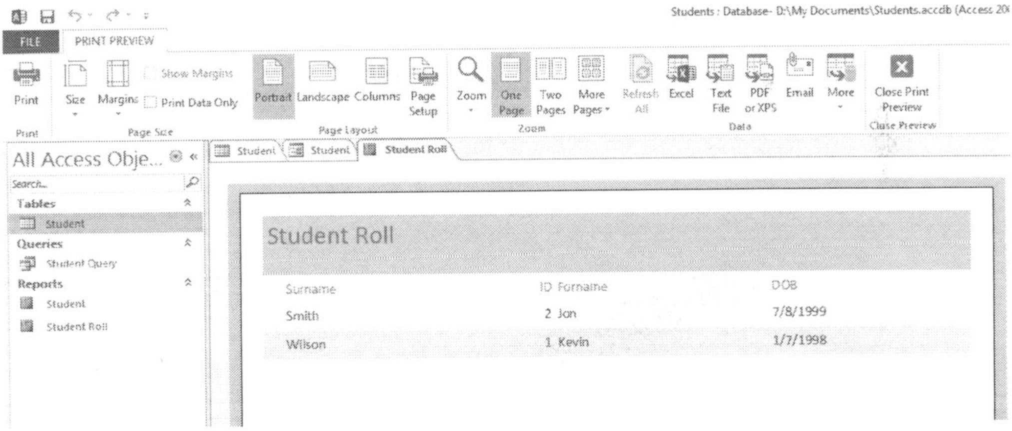

Macros are mini-programs that automate custom tasks. Macros are a simple way to get custom results.

Modules are files that contain Visual Basic code. You can use this code to do just about anything...

Creating a Database

Click the "Blank desktop database" template

Type a file name for the database you're about to create.

Click the Create button

Once the new database has opened, you'll see the home screen. The first thing to take note of are the ribbons at the top of the screen. These contain your tools for working.

The Ribbons

All your tools for creating databases are sorted into ribbons across the top of the screen according to their function.

Home

Clipboard, Sort & Filter, Records, Find, and Text Formatting

Create

Templates, New Tables, Queries, Forms, Reports, and Macros & Code

External Data

Import & Link to other databases, data sources or database servers

Database Tools

Macro, Entity Relationships, Analyse, Move Data, and Add-Ins

Creating Tables

A table is a collection of records. A record contains information about a single item or entity. In a Student table, each record would represent an individual student with name, address, date of birth etc.

Each record is subdivided into fields. Each field stores a bit of the data. For example you'd have a field for student name, one for address, one for date of birth etc.

Each field can be assigned a data type. For example a students name is text, their date of birth is a date, their ID could be a number, their tuition fee is currency, and so on.

Newly created tables get an ID field automatically. The ID field stores a unique number for each record. This is known as a primary key. In the example, the key or ID could be student number.

Microsoft Access automatically creates the first table for you.

To add your fields, click where it says 'click to add', from the drop down box select the data type. So the first field is going to be the student's Forename so the data type will be short text. Once selected enter 'forename'

Do the same for adding surname

For Date of Birth, select the date & time data type

For Address select long text as it will be more than one line of text.

Once you have created all your fields you can go into design view for the table to tweak or change any of the fields and data types you have created.

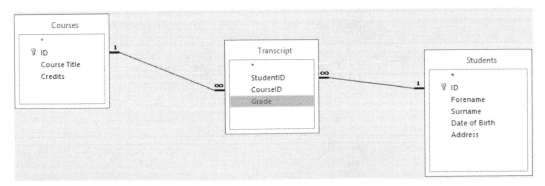

To go into design view, right click on the table name on the left hand side of the screen

Relationships Between Tables

Each table in the database is related to the other tables. In our student database, the students table holds data on students, the courses table holds data on courses but nothing on students. The transcript table holds the results obtained by the students. All this data needs to be related somehow. This is where entity relationships come in.

The relationships are linked using the ID called the primary key (indicated by the little key symbol next to the field).

Relationships can be one-to-one or one-to-many. For example a student takes more than one (or many) courses. So the relationship is one-to-many.

Entering Data

You can enter data directly into the tables as shown in this section, it's just a matter of adding the data to the fields to create the records.

You can also create a form to create a more user friendly interface to enter your data. We will take a look at that in the next section.

Lets take a quick look at adding simple records to a table.

Adding Records

To enter data start typing it into the fields as shown below. Access will automatically add a new record each time you add a name.

	ID	Forename	Surname	Date of Birth	Address	Click to Add
+	1	Kevin	Wilson	01/01/1998	21 Barclay Roa	
+	2	Jon	Smith	05/09/1999	69 Lancaster w	
+	3	Claire	Wilson	06/12/1999	8 Janson Drive	
+	4	Sophie				
*	(New)					

Deleting Records

Right click on the record by clicking the grey border on the left side of the record.

From the popup menu that appears select delete record.

	ID	Forename	Surname	Date of Birth	Address	Click to Add
+	1	Kevin	Wilson	01/01/1998	21 Barclay Roa	
+	2	Jon	Smith	05/09/1999	69 Lancaster w	
+	3	Claire	Wilson	06/12/1999	8 Janson Drive	

- New Record
- Delete Record
- Cut
- Copy
- Paste
- Row Height...

To Resize a Field

Sometimes the data is too long to be able to read it, eg the address fields are quite long. So it helps to widen the column a bit. To do this place your cursor over the right grid-line in the field title. Your mouse will become a double arrow.

	ID		Forename		Surname		Date of Birth		Address		Click to Ad
⊞	1		Kevin		Wilson		01/01/1998		21 Barclay Road		
⊞	2		Jon		Smith		05/09/1999		69 Lancaster Way		
⊞	3		Claire		Wilson		06/12/1999		8 Janson Drive		
⊞	4		Sophie								
∗	(New)										

Now click and drag the line to the right.

Creating Forms

Forms allow you to create a user interface and form the basis of the data entry for your database records.

This helps to simplify things and make them more user friendly as you may have seen from the previous section adding data directly to a table can be tricky. Forms provide a familiar looking interface where the user can enter data into the tables.

A form containing data from the tables created earlier might look like this

As you can see if you compare the form to the table on the opposite page the fields are the same but presented in a more user friendly way with one record at a time. This allows data to be entered and retrieved quickly.

Forms Wizard

The quickest way to create a form is to use the forms wizard. You can find this on the create ribbon

In this example I am going to create a form for entering course information into our database.

Select the courses table on the left hand side.

Then from the create ribbon, select form wizard.

Next follow the instructions on the screen. Select the fields you want by clicking the available fields on the left hand box and click the arrow pointing to the right to add the field.

Next select the layout of the form you want.

Columnar arranges the fields under one another (use this in example)
Tabular arranges the fields next to one another
Datasheet arranges the fields into a table

Give the form a meaningful name

Click finish

Creating Queries

Queries are a set of commands for retrieving data from one or more tables in the database.

When you build a query in Access, you are defining specific search conditions to find exactly the data you want.

For this example I want to create a query that will show me the results of all the students.

First select design query from the create ribbon. Then select the tables you require fields from

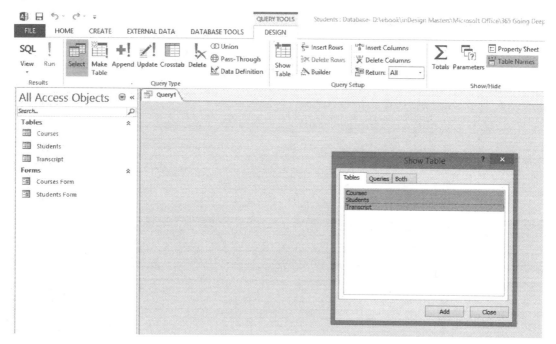

For this query to work I need fields from students table; students name, I need fields from the courses table; course name, and fields from the transcript table; the results. So highlight all the tables in the dialog box.

So by double clicking on the fields I need, I can build my query

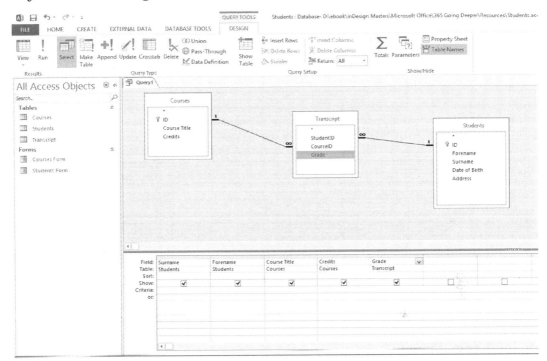

When you are done, click run, top left of your screen. You will see the results of your new query.

Forename	Surname	Course Title	Credits	Grade
Kevin	Wilson	Understanding Computer Hardw	120	A
Kevin	Wilson	Fundamentals of Office 365	120	C
Kevin	Wilson	Biology 101	120	B
Jon	Smith	Fundamentals of Office 365	120	C
Jon	Smith	Biology 101	120	A
Jon	Smith	Understanding Computer Hardw	120	D

Creating Reports

Reports allow you to quickly display your data in printable form. This could be for income and expenses reports, names and addresses, student results, etc depending on what data your database stores. These can all be printed off or even emailed.

To create a report, click your data source from the Access Objects listed down the left hand side of your screen then click the Create ribbon.

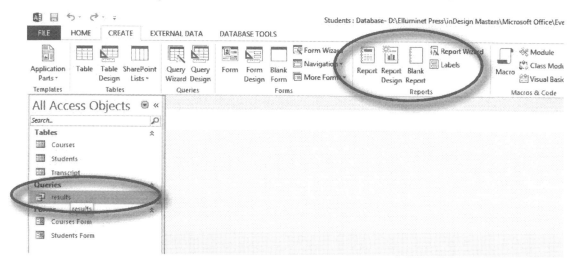

Report will automatically create report with all of the data from your table or query. This is the simplest report, Access will not structure or group any of the data.

Blank Report & Blank Design will create an empty canvas where you can manually add the fields you want and lay them out according to your own design.

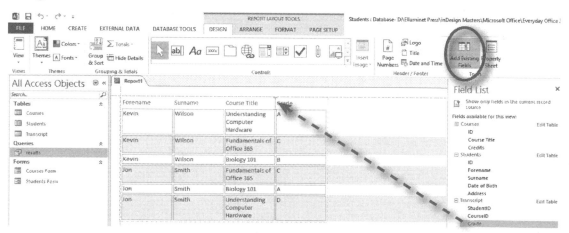

Click 'Add Existing Fields' and from the list drag the fields to your report as shown above.

Report Wizard guides you through the report creation process, allowing to select the fields from your chosen source.

To create a report using the wizard, first select your data source from the 'Access Objects' listed down the left hand side. Reports are usually created from queries so in the student example, select the 'results' query.

From the create ribbon select report wizard.

From the dialog box that appears, select the fields. For this particular report I want to show a list of students and the results they got for their classes.

To do this I need the fields surname, forename, course title and grade.

Show how you want to show your data. The results are presented per student so in this case I will show them by student

So in this case, the student's name is printed followed by a list of their results.

Click next, then finish when you get to the end of the wizard.

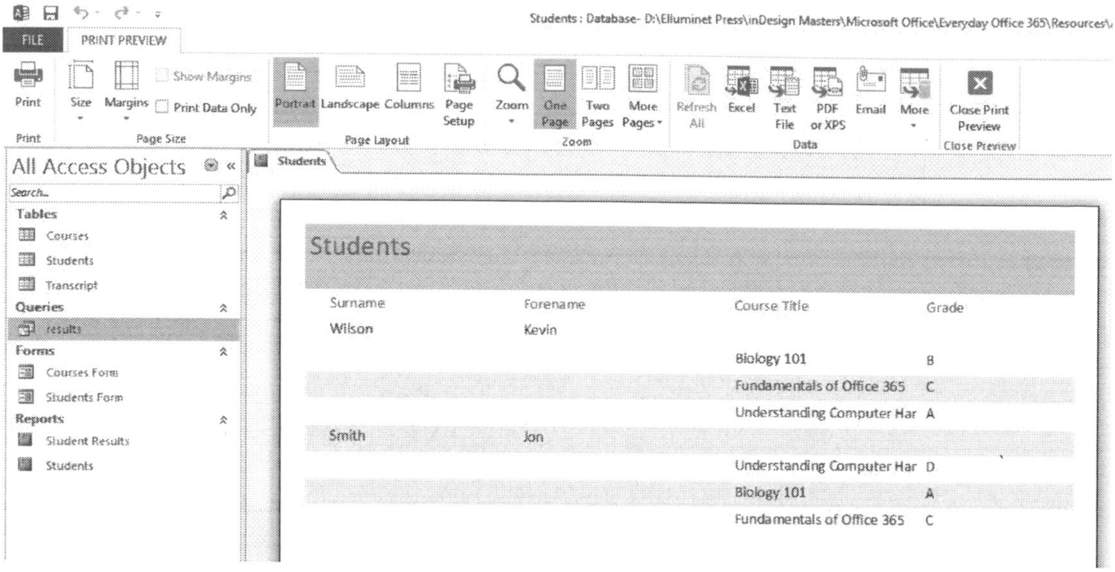

Microsoft Outlook 2016

Microsoft Outlook 2016 is a personal information manager and email application available as a part of the Microsoft Office suite. It includes a calendar, contact list or address book as well as the ability to set reminders and make notes.

Outlook 2016 can be used as a stand-alone application for a personal email account, or can work with Microsoft Exchange for multiple users in an organization, such as shared mailboxes and calendars, public folders and meeting schedules.

Outlook 2016 organizes your email, calendars and contacts all in one place. It all starts with your email account.

From there you can start working with email, composing messages and replying to them. Storing the addresses of the people you interact with in your contacts, so you never have to remember an email address or phone number.

Also dealing with junk mail and clutter.

Let's start by taking a quick look at the basics.

Getting Started with Outlook

When you start Outlook you will see the main screen. In the following screen I've highlighted the main features in order to get started quickly and easily.

I find it a good idea to turn the reading pane off on your inbox. This helps with security so Outlook doesn't automatically open unknown emails.

Select your inbox on the left hand side. Go to your view ribbon, click 'reading pane' and in the drop down box select 'off'.

This will remove the reading pane. To open any email, double click on the message and it will open in a separate window.

I have found it useful, if you receive a lot of email. You can set Outlook to show only unread emails or all emails.

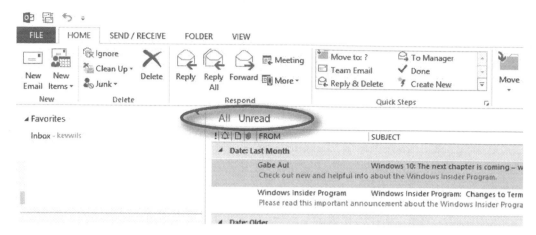

If you click 'Unread' Outlook will only show email you have not opened.

Main Ribbon Menus

All the main features and functions of Outlook are divided up into tabs called ribbons.

File Ribbon

This is where you can find all your printing, saving, import and account settings.

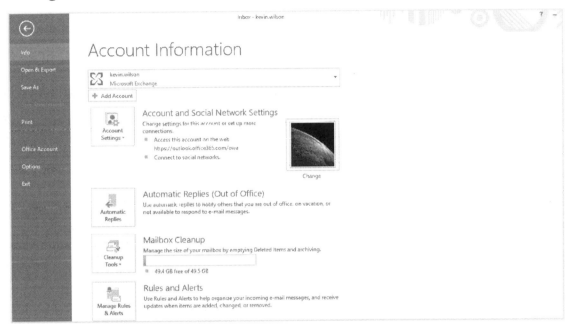

Home Ribbon

This is where you will find all your most used features such as composing new emails, reply and delete functions.

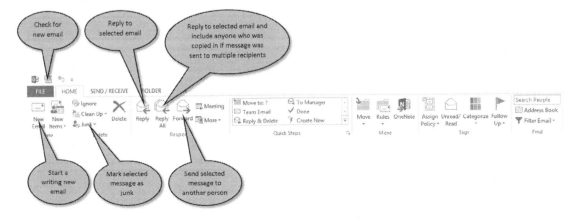

Send/Receive Ribbon

This is where you will find all your functions for manual sending and receiving email.

Most of the time you won't need to use these except when you want to manually check for new emails, etc.

Folder Ribbon

The folder ribbon is where you will find functions to create folders for organizing your emails.

For example, perhaps a folder for "Vicki" for all email from Vicki, or folder for "Accounts" for all email from accounting/banking, etc.

Or all your in-boxes if you have multiple email accounts, all listed under favourites.

To do this, click the 'show in favourites' icon.

View Ribbon

The view ribbon allows you to sort your emails by name or date and allows you to turn on or off different sections, such as the reading pane.

Email Message Ribbons

When you go to reply to an email message or compose a new one you will find that the message window has its own set of ribbons.

Message Ribbon

This ribbon shows up when you have opened an email message either to reply to one you have received or one you are composing.

You can find all your common formatting tools here such as fonts, colours, text alignments etc. As well as address books and file attachments.

Insert Ribbon

Use this ribbon if you want to insert shapes, charts, tables, calendar appointments, hyper-links or any kind of symbol.

Options Ribbon

Use this ribbon to enable the BCC field, set up delivery reports, page colours and effects.

Format Text Ribbon

Use this ribbon to format your text.

To change fonts, align text left or right, change font size, change line or paragraph indent, create bullet and numbered lists, etc

Review Ribbon

The review ribbon has features to check spelling and grammar. It also has statistical features such as word counts.

You can lookup certain words and find synonyms for words using a thesaurus.

Translate into different languages etc.

Sending Email

From the home ribbon click New E-mail.

In the window that appears enter the email address of your recipient in the To field. You can do this by typing in the address and Outlook will search your contacts and display suggested addresses.

You can also add email addressed by clicking the To field and selecting the recipients from your address book. Note you can select more than one if you want to send the same message to other people.

The Cc field is for carbon copies and is used to send a copy of the message to other people.

The Bcc field is for blind carbon copies - you can enable this on the options ribbon if it isn't there. This works like the CC field except the recipient can't see the addresses of the other people the message has been sent to.

Then type your message in at the bottom.

Attachments

You can also send attachments, such as photos or documents. To do this click on the Attach File icon that looks like a paper clip.

When you click 'attach file', Outlook will list your most recently used documents.

More often than not the file you want to attach is in this list. To attach it, just click on the file in the list. If not click 'browse this PC'.

Select your file from the insert file dialog box and click insert. You can select more than one file by holding down the control (ctrl) key on your keyboard.

Click insert.

Once you are happy with your message, click Send.

Improvements include: the ability to attach most recent files intuitively, improved cloud attachment features, ability to change file permissions within the email attachment.

Calendar

To start your Calendar, click the calendar icon located at the bottom left of your screen.

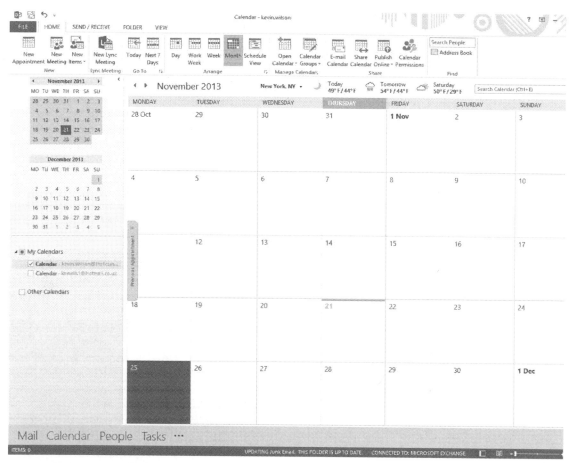

Once you are in your calendar you can see the calendar with months and dates. It is personal preference but I find it easier to work within month view.

You can do this by clicking on the month icon on your home ribbon shown as shown above.

Add Appointment

The quickest way to add an event or appointment is to double click the day.

So, for example, if you wanted to add an appointment on the 25th, double click 25.

The following dialog appears, Remove the tick from "all day event" this will allow you to enter specific times; start time and estimated finishing times.

Click 'Save & Close' when you have finished.

In the screen above you can see the appointment has been added.

Dealing with Junk Mail

If you have been using the internet you will no doubt have received junk mail in the past. Mail advertising products from unknown senders that you wonder how they got your email address.

Outlook has a junk mail filter. It is good practice to enable this filter as suspicious emails used for phishing personal details, etc.

To enable the filter click 'junk' from the home ribbon

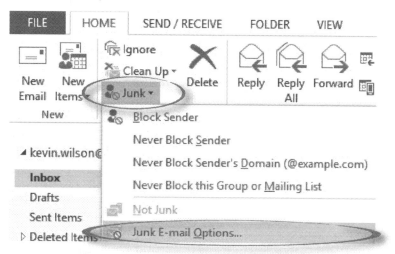

In the dialog box that pops up select 'low: move the most obvious junk email to the junk email folder'

Also select 'disable links...' and 'warn about suspicious domains...'.

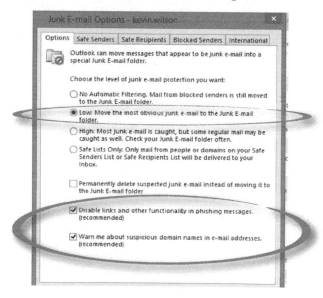

This helps to filter out emails sent from scammers etc.

All these emails will be filtered into your junk mail box instead of your inbox.

Clutter

Clutter is available for business users and at the time of writing is only available on certain Office 365 subscriptions.

You can enable clutter by right clicking on the clutter folder in Outlook.

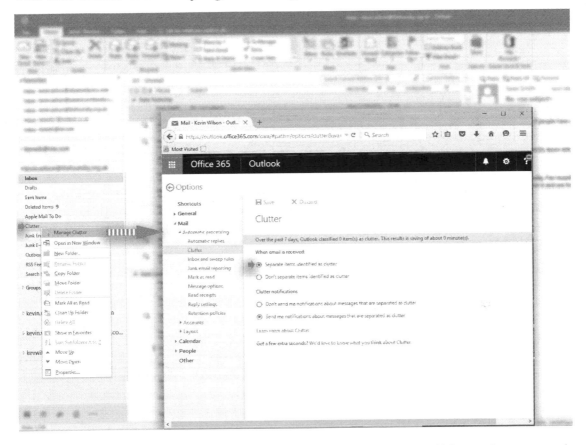

In the menu that appears, select 'manage clutter'. This will launch your web browser and take you to Microsoft Online where you will need to log in with your Microsoft Account details.

Chapter 12

Microsoft OneNote

Microsoft OneNote is a digital note taking application and allows you to type notes, draw annotations on touch screen devices, add website clippings, photos and images.

This app is a cut down touch oriented version of Microsoft Office OneNote 2016 that comes with Office 2016 Suite.

Getting Started

Opening OneNote you'll see the home screen with the ribbon menus across the top.

Down the left hand side you will see a list of notes.

Tools are organised into ribbons.

Home Ribbon

On the home ribbon you'll find your most commonly used tools; **bold**, *italic*, underlined text, bullets and numbered lists, indentations for paragraphs and lines, to do list check marks, paragraph alignment (left, right and centred) as well as inserting pictures.

Insert Ribbon

The insert ribbon will allow you to insert tables, attach a downloaded file, insert a picture or add a website link.

Draw Ribbon

From the draw ribbon you can select tools to make handwritten notes and annotations. You can select from coloured pens and highlighters as well as different colours.

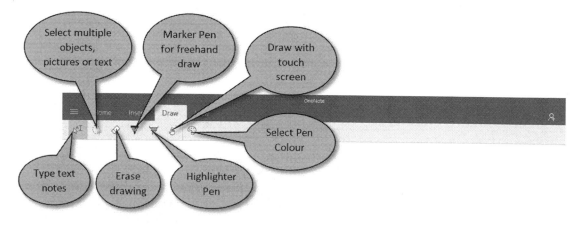

View Ribbon

The view ribbon will allow you to zoom in and out of your notebook pages. You can also enable your ruled lines if you are hand writing notes these can be a helpful guide.

Taking Notes

You can take notes in a variety of ways, use annotated web pages, pictures, handwritten or typed notes.

Edge Browser

With Windows 10 and OneNote you can use Microsoft Edge web browser's annotation features to make notes on a web page and save them as notes.

Make your annotations using Microsoft Edge's annotation feature, then tap the disk icon along the top of the tool bar. Tap 'OneNote' then 'add'.

Once you have saved them as a note, the notes will appear in your OneNote App.

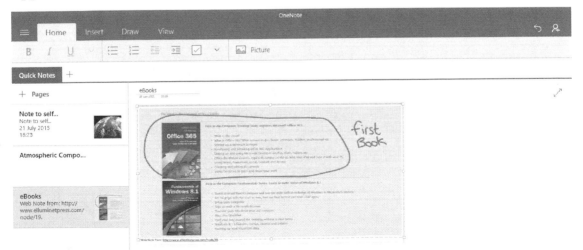

Pictures

To insert pictures or photographs, make sure you tap the note you want the image to appear then from the home ribbon tap 'picture'

From the dialogue box that appears, choose the image you want and tap 'open'.

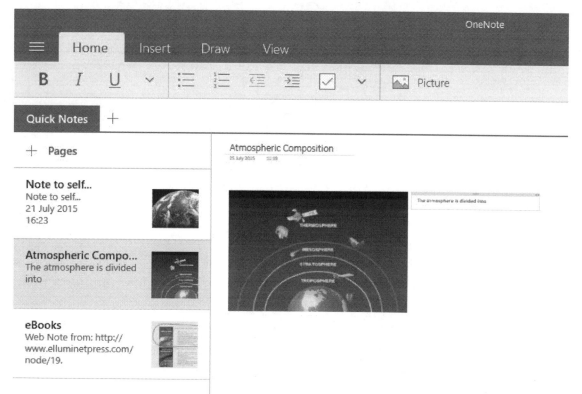

Tables

To insert tables, make sure you tap on the note you want the table to appear, then from the insert ribbon tap 'table'.

Your table will appear in your note. You can drag the table to the position you want it. Tap in the cells to enter your data.

To add more columns use the tab key on the on screen keyboard or tap the table ribbon and tap 'insert right' to add another column on the end.

Similarly to add rows hit your enter key or from the table ribbon tap 'insert below' to add a row.

Write Notes

You can handwrite notes and annotations using either your finger or a stylus. Tap on the draw ribbon along the top of your screen. From this ribbon you'll see a number of tools.

The first two icons are to select objects. You can use these to select and move your text boxes, photos, annotations etc. You also have an eraser, thin marker, highlighter, draw with finger and your colour pallet to change the colour of your pen.

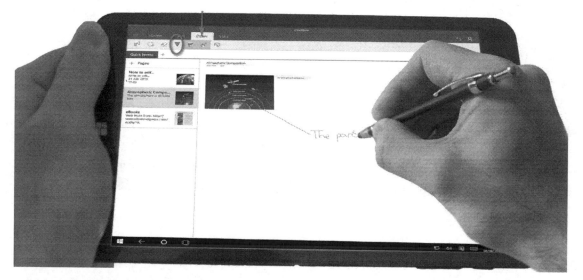

You can change the colour of your pen by tapping on the pallet icon on the draw ribbon

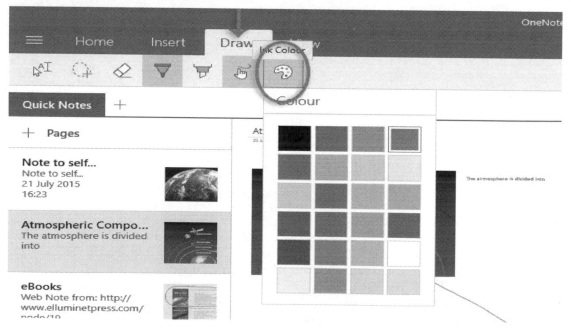

Type Notes

You can also type notes by tapping on the screen where you want your note to appear and on the keyboard that appears type your information

Using Tags

You can tag parts of your notes. This helps you to organise and prioritise notes and to do lists. You can tag things as important (illustrated with a star) or as critical so you can mark things you need to do right away or to highlight.

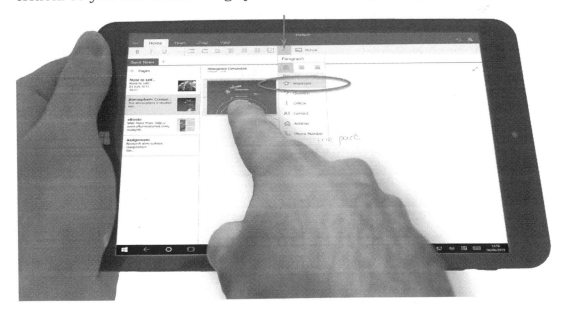

ToDo List

You can create to-do lists in your notes by tapping on your text box entering your note then tapping the to-do list icon on the home ribbon.

This will add a square check box next to the note. You can also mark these check boxes as 'done' by tapping on the check box. This will add a small tick.

Office Lens

Office Lens turns your smartphone or tablet into a scanner. With this scanner you can scan documents, business cards, receipts, sticky notes, whiteboards and other real-world items into your OneNote.

In this example I am going to use an iPhone but you can use Lens on your tablet, or phone.

First you need to download the Office Lens app from the app store. From the search field type 'office lens'. Tap 'office lens' in the list. Tap the Office Lens icon and tap 'get'. Once it has download and installed tap Office Lens on your home screen.

Once Office Lens has opened, sign in with your Microsoft Account email address and password.

At the bottom of the screen you will see a choice of different objects you can scan: business cards, allows you to scan a business card and add the details to your contacts; photo; document; whiteboard, that allows you to scan writing on a whiteboard and add it to OneNote.

In this example I am going to scan a business card. Swipe across the list at the bottom of your screen and select 'business card'.

Take a picture of the card by tapping the orange button.

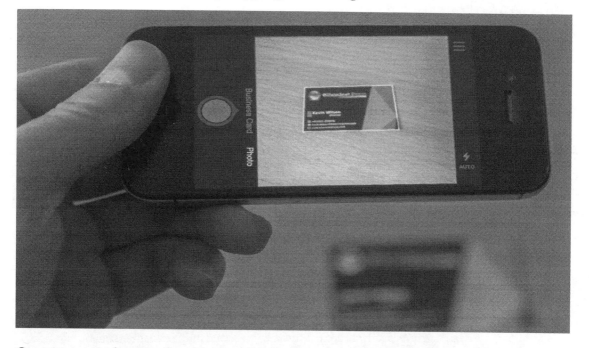

Once you are happy that the card is in focus, tap 'done' on the top right of the screen.

Tap on 'OneNote (Contact + Image) and enter a name.

Tap on the name you just gave your business card scan (in this example 'publisher').

OneNote has created a new note containing the business card image and extracted contact details.

OneNote has also created a contact list entry and added the details from the business card (phone, email address and website) to your address book.

You can do the same with written notes, whiteboard notes, photos, etc.

Made in the USA
Lexington, KY
24 December 2015